What others are saying

If you want to read a powerful message about hope, dealing with adversity and overcoming perceived bad situations I strongly recommend this book. If you are looking for a message to deliver to your athletes, students or administration this is it.

Mitchell Tomaszkiewicz
Sports Information Director and
Head Cross Country Coach at Suny Coblesill N.Y.

Read with anticipation about Brian's experiences on his road as a father, a son, a husband, a friend and a quadriplegic. Begin to construct your path by standing on Brian's stumbling blocks/ lessons to help lift you on your road. Understand how Rising UP, is not just getting UP, Rising UP is purposeful, repeatable, and will work for you. Brian keeps it simple, defines what is important, walks you through an experience that will open you to Rising UP, find out how.

Kevin Bracken
American Greco-Roman wrestler who competed in the 2000
Summer Olympics. Owner Olympian Wrestling Club, Castle
Rock, Co.

If you read one book this summer make sure it's this one! Brian's insight and wisdom on the topic of Rising UP are wonderful. This is s must read!

Kevin Brown
COO The King's College New York,
and former assistant to the president at Focus on the Family

Rising Up
By Brian P. Swift

Copyright © 2018 by Brian P. Swift

Printed and Electronic Versions
ISBN-13: 978-0-9981194-5-8
(Brian P. Swift /Motivation Champs)

The book was printed in the United States of America. To order additional copies, bulk order, or book speaking engagements contact:
www.brianpswift.com

Or You May, Contact the Publisher, Motivation Champs Publishing. www.motivationchamps.com

Acknowledgments

To the hundreds of motivators around the
world who have made an impact on me,
my vision and my journey.
You have enriched my life and helped teach me wisdom.
My eyes have been opened to all the blessings
I have been privileged to receive.

To TO, KB, JS, MD, DD and all those
who have strengthened my faith.

Thank you, and God bless

Thank you to:

God, who has given me an extraordinary life.

My mom and dad, Alice and Bud, and my two sisters,
Kathy and Karen, for their endless support, love and faith.

My amazing wife Monica, words cannot even begin to
describe her selfless acts and sacrifices.

My three heartbeats, Spencer, Sydney and Callaghan.

In loving memory of Einstein, my service dog.

RISING UP

Gain Perspective, Vision, and Passion

Thank you for purchasing this book!

A portion of the proceeds will be donated to Swift Outdoor Accessible Recreation (SOAR) a 501(c) (3) nonprofit organization.

The mission of Swift Outdoor Accessible Recreation is to offer programs and services for individuals with disabilities that promote being close to nature. Brian Swift founded Swift Outdoor Accessible Recreation (SOAR) in 2015. At age 17, Brian Swift received an injury while playing football that damaged his spine. Since the accident, he has been a quadriplegic. He has never let his disability keep him from achieving his goals and participating in activities he loves.

People with disabilities often receive fewer opportunities for physical exercise and outdoor activities than do others. SOAR strives to offer our participants a wide variety of therapeutic recreation focused on enhancing lives both mentally and physically.

Therapeutic recreation has been shown to reduce pain, depression, stress, and anxiety while at the same time increasing strength, endurance, flexibility, and self-esteem. Therapeutic recreation also enhances social skills, self-advocacy skills, and independence while also improving mental alertness, attention span, and problem solving.

Lack of outdoor play and activity has been correlated with negative psychological and physical effects including obesity, loneliness, depression, attention problems, and greater social isolation due to reduced time with friends and family.

Find out more at soarnonprofit.com

CONTENTS

Why This Book is Important for YOU......................... 1

A Note from the Author 3

Chapter 1   It's Your Time 9

Chapter 2   Fundamentals of Success 19

Chapter 3   Power of One................................ 29

Chapter 4   Wisdom vs. Knowledge 35

Chapter 5   Positive Choices................................ 41

Chapter 6   Leadership.................................... 49

Chapter 7   Be Significant 57

Chapter 8   Emotions 65

Chapter 9   Ups and Downs and Downs and
             Ups and Downs 79

Chapter 10   Paying the Price 89

Chapter 11   Attitude 95

Chapter 12   The Beat Down 103

Chapter 13   Moving Forward with Purpose........... 113

Chapter 14   Getting Up 119

Notes   125

Suggested Additional Reading 129

Why This Book is Important for YOU

This book is focused on teaching you how to overcome the obstacles that are holding you back from being the best version of you and from living the richest life you can live.

Within these covers, it is my goal to help you learn new ways to succeed in spite of the UPS and DOWNS that life can sometimes throw in our path. I want you to know that you can RISE UP after your setbacks and be better than ever as a result.

This book is written with the express purpose of helping you create your best life! Join me as we get there together.

A Note from the Author

"Don't tell me the sky's the limit
when there are footprints on the moon!"
Paul Brandt

My life hit the cross roads when I was 17. I broke my neck while playing football with my friends on the day after Christmas, 1979. As I found the courage and strength to recover, I graduated from high school, started my 22-year coaching career at a catholic grammar school, Saint Albert the Great, in Burbank, Illinois, earned my college degree, and my Juris Doctor degree as a quadriplegic. I also found my purpose: to achieve more than expected, and to aspire to be the best I could.

I am a wheelchair user with a spinal cord injury. Similar to many others I have met in this situation, I am not sad, angry or depressed. However, unlike some others I have met, I do not ponder *the why* of my situation, as I presume there is a reason beyond my comprehension.

It is very common for people to think that the thing I want the most in life is to walk. Actually, I have not prayed or asked God to make me walk. Instead, I have asked for the strength and courage to live a life of significance. I believe that things happen for a reason. People cross paths for a reason. Some people will fill our life with motivation and possibilities and some people will only make a small impact. Some people will become friends and some will remain acquaintances. No matter what, the thing I want to impart to you today is the necessity to continue to rise up and keep moving forward. Absorb the knowledge and share the wisdom you learned from the experiences and people that have come through your life. You were meant to make a significant impact and influence others in this lifetime and my hope is that this book will motivate you to rise up and move forward toward that goal.

I don't think that our society in general, even medical professionals, know enough about the physical and psychological impact of spinal cord injuries. Of course, neither did I nor my family and friends prior to my accident. Perceptions are formed through the common examples of seeing someone in a wheelchair, designated ramps, automatic doors, and parking spots in our neighborhoods. Possibly, you have a personal connection to someone affected by paralysis. However, much of their story cannot be seen or understood.

As a quadriplegic of 38 years, I am constantly reminded that I am lucky to be alive and I am fully aware that paralysis alone will not kill me. The secondary conditions of paralysis, especially without steadfast management, can kill me. An injured spinal cord struggles to or simply cannot communicate with the brain to operate a host of bodily functions most of us take for granted.

Explaining that I cannot walk is not the challenge, as my wheelchair telegraphs that fact to the people I meet. But, explaining that my body cannot regulate temperature, sexual function, bladder or bowel function, without some combination of supplements, medication, equipment, and strict timetables is much more difficult to explain given the general public's current level of awareness.

For me, the most difficult part of living with a spinal cord injury is the loss of control and being robbed of time. When I broke my neck, I did not simply lose my ability to walk, I lost my ability to control my autonomic functions. The ongoing management of body temperature, sexual function, bladder and bowel steal hours off my days. It also comes at a cost to my wife, children, family, and friends.

A lot of people don't want to discuss the graphic details of the acts that happen in the bedroom or the bathroom, or the act of spasming or not sleeping night after night. Most people go through their daily routine with these actions simply being a part of daily life.

Managing my secondary conditions is a full-time job, and even with close scrutiny, can get the better of me. Managing these secondary conditions always seems to come with a sacrifice, loss or penalty. In the pursuit of a healthy and active lifestyle, those of us living with spinal cord injuries are forced to invest significantly higher sums of time and money for a shot at opportunity.

The toll of secondary conditions becomes a daily adversary. I am not looking for sympathy or praise, as I have been blessed to have as much in common with people without disabilities as I do with people with disabilities. However, there is no benefit in denying that any physical activity I engage in takes me longer, costs me more, and strains my body to a greater extent, especially as time passes.

Truth be told, all of us in wheelchairs dream of getting up and out of our wheelchairs. I imagine most of us also dream about simply reclaiming control of our bodies. However, through all my years of being a quadriplegic, I am strong because I had to be, smart because of my mistakes, happier because of the sadness I have known, and now wiser because I learned one of the best feelings in the world is when you can truly say I did the hard work.

I know firsthand what it's like to be confined by physical adversity. However, we are all confined in some way whether by a physical or emotional injury sustained in this life. My confinement is easy to spot but for many people dealing with emotional injuries, their confinement is not as easily recognized. I want to help you turn your roadblocks into building blocks. I want people to get off the sidelines and into the game of life and make a difference.

I quickly realized that many of the lessons and philosophies that guided me as a coach equally applied to life. As a young man, I was driven to read. I read books about and by great coaches. I wanted to learn how to coach, inspire, motivate, develop and lead.

I read books by many of the great coaches including, but in no way limited to, Lou Holtz, John McKay, Lloyd Carr, Pete Carroll, Ara Parseghian, Knute Rockne, Urban Meyer, Joe Paterno, Paul "Bear" Bryant, Lou Carnesecca, John Calipari, Rick Pitino, Dean Smith, Bobby Knight, Mike Krzyzewski and John Wooden. I also read books by some of the great NFL and NBA coaches and players.

I realized in order to grow myself, I had to first know myself. My burning desire has always been to make a difference in people's lives and to become the best person I can be. The end goal has always been to be a good husband, father, mentor, son, brother and friend. Now the proud father of three and the most blessed husband for more than 29 years, I have developed a strategy of success, CIA: Commitment, Integrity and Attitude.

For me, another way of looking at the work that must be done, is to gain the power of RISING UP! RISING UP can be can be explained, demonstrated and defined in so many ways! The two-letter word UP has more meanings than any other two-letter word in the English language. It is listed in the dictionary as an adverb, preposition, adjective, noun, and a verb.

It's easy to understand UP, when it means toward the sky or at the top of the list. But then again, in the morning, we wake UP. It takes courage to speak UP. We can call UP our friends, we can brighten UP a room, polish UP silver, warm UP leftovers, and clean UP the kitchen. We lock UP the house and fix UP the old car. People stir UP trouble, line UP for tickets, work UP an appetite, and think UP excuses. To be dressed is one thing, but to be dressed UP is special. We open UP a store in the morning, but we close it UP at night.

This little word UP has many diverse meanings, and if you're UP to it, you might try building UP a list of many ways it is used. It will take UP a lot of your time, but if you don't give UP, you may wind UP with 100 or more ways you could use the word UP. You might even create a riddle: "What is the first thing you do in the morning and the last thing you do at night?"

U   P

Did I crack you UP?

Honestly, my heartfelt desire in writing this book and sharing my story is for you to know that while you cannot control everything that happens to you in your own life, you CAN control how you respond. Your response is your sUPer power.

By the time you reach the last page of this book, I intend to provide you with the information you need to be invigorated to face your own struggles with hope, faith, and purpose! You have all the tools you need to overcome any obstacle, to get back on track, and get UP especially when the task at hand seems insurmountable. My goal is to help you unearth those tools that have always been within you. You need to dig deep inside yourself and find that "something" that makes a difference.

My quest as a writer started one day when a friend of mine said something important to me. I took it as one of the biggest compliments, the biggest burden, and the biggest obligation I currently have to live up to!

He said: "I thought of you when I read this:

'A real man is the kind of man
that when your feet hit the floor each morning
the devil says Oh Crap, he's up!'

To the cool man that has touched my life. Here's to you!! A real Brother walks with you when the rest of the world walks on you. I LOVE YA BROTHER!"

CHAPTER 1

IT'S YOUR TIME

My life changed when I took accountability and stopped looking outside for motivation and inspiration. I learned to motivate and inspire myself by always being open to learn, striving for more, taking action, being grateful and strengthening my faith. If you are struggling to move forward in your life, the trick is to take responsibility for motivating and developing yourself. Stop leaving that in the hands of others!

I have many passions, some of which are to coach, develop, and assist those who want to dig deep and challenge themselves. If you are reading this, I may be describing you. All of us have been given the power and the tools to live our lives to the fullest while helping others achieve their dreams. The process is easier than you may think and I can guide you on the journey of your lifetime. I challenge you to discover your personal potential and your innate ability to accomplish all of your goals. It is all within your reach. I have finally learned that the way YOU get what you want is by working on your own self-improvement each day and then helping others get what they want.

It's your time! Everyone has the potential for greatness. You have a gift to offer to the world. It is the ability to make the most of yourself and then to use that to encourage others to do the same. Every day is an opportunity to be a more powerful, optimistic, successful, and significant. You are meant to shine and to do wonderful things.

A successful and significantly happy life will only occur if you go for it. All of us have heard that, but living it every day is not easy. Actually, there are many times it is extremely difficult. Life is a journey, and it's never too late to decide that it is your time to make it what you have always wanted it to be. This lifestyle of being significant is a journey worth committing to.

I don't know who said this phrase first, but I used it all the time while managing my sales teams. It is "paralysis by analysis". We have a tendency to do this all the time when we are unsure about how to move forward or whenever we become aware that some things are not working as we planned and we feel like we are losing control. We procrastinate so as not to rock the boat any further. We feel this is a safe option because by doing nothing, nothing will get any worse. What we fail to realize is that by doing nothing we are creating a monstrous gap between where we are and where we want to go. This is the time we need to stop over analyzing and instead, take action!

As Victor Kiam is quoted as saying:
"Even if you fall on your face,
You're still moving forward."

Time never stands still. You are either moving closer to your goals or you are moving further away from your goals. Standing still, or as we mentioned earlier, "paralysis by analysis" is not an option if you ever hope to achieve your goals. If you are not moving closer by taking the steps necessary to get there, you are, by default, moving further away from your goals.

Will all the forward moving steps you take be perfect? Absolutely not, and that's OK! It comes down to two choices, you can get better or you can get bitter about your situation. Anyone can learn how to create a better quality of life with this simple three-step recipe.

1. Focus on becoming the best YOU that you can be, physically, mentally and spiritually.
2. Focus on helping others become the best they can be physically, mentally and spiritually.
3. Repeat

If you follow this simple strategy, you will enjoy a blessed, successful and significant life.

Steps Toward Becoming the Best YOU

Creating *your time or the best YOU* requires a commitment to yourself physically, emotionally and spiritually. It requires you to be honest with yourself about where you are now, where you want to be and a willingness to stretch beyond your comfort zone to get there. Through this process, you will find new ways to look at life. By being honest with yourself and willing to listen to the advice given to you by the people in your life who are wiser, you can reach your goals faster. Guidance can come from so many positive people in our lives, including friends, family, coaches, spiritual leaders or God. This requires commitment, integrity and attitude.

There comes a time in your life when you finally get it. You become self-aware and totally honest with yourself. This is when you stop and tell yourself, "ENOUGH!" When you decide the life you are living is not the life you envisioned for yourself and that is the good news! You begin to look at yourself and the world through new eyes. This is your awakening and the sooner you get there, the better because that moment is the first step on your journey toward becoming the best you. This experience can occur numerous times throughout your life, if you are lucky.

My first awakening came the day after Christmas when I was 17 and broke my neck playing football with my friends. Life could have turned ugly, but I was blessed to have strong faithful parents who helped me stay optimistic. Through their words and actions, they reassured me that life was going to work out as long as I worked hard, kept my faith strong and kept moving forward.

This was not going to be easy, being a quadriplegic confined to a wheelchair, but as my dad use to say, "No one promised that life was going to be easy." We have all sat watching that show or commercial on the television about the military training or extreme training like American Ninjas and said to ourselves, "I can do that" or "I think I can do that". After I broke my neck, I had to say that to myself on a daily basis, and mean it! That period of my life was my first opportunity to dig deep and see what I was really made of. It was extremely difficult, but so worth it.

I came to the realization that I was not going to let my wheelchair hold me back. When you are facing your darkest moments, you too will hit that realization the world is not holding you back. In fact, no one is holding you back. Actually, you may be holding the world back, and in doing so, you are holding yourself back. Your potential is endless. Now is the time to expose the superhero that is in all of us. Put your fears aside and grab your cape, put on your special suit, and take action.

You realize it's time to stop hoping and waiting for something to change, or for happiness, safety and security to magically appear over the next horizon. No one, other than YOU, is going to give you permission to rise above the rest, to be successful and shine. That power to change was yours yesterday, it is yours today and it will be yours tomorrow. As soon as you recognize that, you will be well on your way to becoming the best YOU there is.

You realize that in the real world there isn't always sunshine and rainbows and that any chance of "happily ever after" must begin and end with you. It isn't about the rat race or having money, fame, and popularity. It's not about what you have; it's about what you do with what you have.

You awaken to the fact that you are not perfect, you make mistakes, and that not everyone will always love, appreciate or approve of who or what you are, and that's okay. They are entitled to their own views and opinions.

There is a famous quote from Brazilian lyricist and novelist Paulo Coelho:

> *"What other people think of you is none of*
> *your business."*

You learn the importance of championing yourself, and in the process, a sense of control overcomes you which leads to a stronger feeling of confidence and pride. You must be your own advocate, an active participant in creating your future. When you do that, you will naturally start making better decisions and choices, holding yourself more accountable and as a result, turn your dreams into reality.

You stop complaining and blaming other people for the things they did to you, or didn't do for you. You learn that the only person you can really count on is you, and if you are truly blessed, family, a few close friends and your faith.

The lessons presented are often completely different from those you think you need. Life's lessons do not come in nice neat little packages. Growth and learning wisdom is a process of trial and error and experimentation. You can learn as much from failure as you can success. Actually, I believe you learn more from failing than you do from succeeding.

It was Thomas A. Edison who, when asked about his disastrous light bulb experiments, said:

> *"I have not failed.*
> *I've just found 10,000 ways that won't work."*
> Thomas A. Edison

Lessons will be presented to you in various forms until you have learned them. When you see the challenges in your life change, it will be your indicator that your attitude and behavior have also changed as once you have learned the lesson, you will move on to the next lesson. Learning lessons is a journey not a destination.

Every stage of life contains some lessons. As long as you live, there will be something more to learn, something more to experience. What you make of your life is up to you. You can either choose to be an active participant in the daily creation of your life or you can be an idle passenger. Either way, the clock is ticking and time is moving forward with or without you. If your life is not as you wish it could be, you have likely forgotten that you have all the tools and resources you need to create your best life. Throughout this book, I will remind you of those tools and how you can use them to enjoy your best life. The question is simple: when you know you have all the tools you need to create your best life, will you? Remember that through faith, desire, goal-setting and unwavering effort you can have anything you want.

Goal Setting and Goal Achieving

Self-discipline is your secret weapon when it comes to achieving your goals. We need to constantly encourage and re-assure ourselves that what we are doing is all worthwhile. There is nothing worse than living with regret due to lack of self-discipline. Being disciplined is hard, but living with regret is harder.

> Stephen R. Covey reminds us,
> *"The price of discipline is always less than the pain of regret."*

Do whatever it takes to remind yourself that it's your time. Our lives are full of these reminders. At the University of Notre Dame before the football players take the field, they touch a sign that says, "PLAY LIKE A CHAMPION TODAY." This is just a last-minute reminder for the team, a checkup from the neck up. It is a confirmation of everything they have worked and sacrificed for.

My checkup from the neck up consists of numerous quotes. When I would train for long wheelchair rides I knew I needed more motivation and inspiration to keep me going when I hit that breaking point. I suggest you start to build your own list of inspirational/motivational quotes that resonate with you. I wore a wristband that has the inscription "IRONMAN" on it. I started wearing it 20 years ago after watching a special about Dick Hoyt and his son, Rick who has cerebral palsy.

Dick Hoyt, an amazing man and devoted father, has pushed his disabled son in more than 1000 races including six Ironman triathlons, seven half Ironman triathlons, 31 Boston Marathons and over 255 triathlons. It is an amazing story about an amazing man and his relationship with his son and their commitment to accomplish something that you only read about in superhero books and see in the movies. I implore you to watch it. You can learn more by visiting their website at: *http://www.teamhoyt. com*. I have seen the documentary numerous times and I have shown it to my kids and to every team I have managed. I guarantee that no matter how much you give, how hard you work, how committed you are, and how spent you feel, when you're finished watching this documentary, you will realize you have so much more inside of you.

Here are three great tools that will help you achieve your goals:
1. Learn to be thankful and to take comfort in many of the simple things that many people take for granted. Things like good health, food to eat, water to drink, a roof over your head, and loving people to share your life.
2. Begin to take responsibility for yourself and make a

promise to never betray yourself and to never, ever settle for less than your heart's desire.

3. Promise yourself that you will never put your life on hold and you will always move forward. If you are passionate enough, you can do what you love for the rest of your life.

We could all do with a little more inspiration in our lives. Times are tough, but tough times don't last; tough people do. Sometimes, it just takes one inspirational line to help us gain some perspective. That little voice in your head called self-talk is often harmful, but it can also be extremely beneficial if you have control of it. When you find yourself being tested, and you will, I recommend you give yourself that checkup from the neck up with positive self-talk.

Success does not always go to the strongest, best educated, or the richest person, but to the person who believes he can. You cannot follow someone else's game plan. You have to figure out your own personal game plan and then promise yourself that you will stick to it. I have provided some practical exercises to help you move forward.

Self-Reflection

1. List up to three (3) areas of self-doubt you have in your life today.

2. Are you where you want to be in your life?

3. What can you do to get over the self-doubt and get closer to what you want to be versus where you are at?

4. Write down what your vision is for your ideal life.

5. Share your vision with three (3) people. Ask them how, or if they think that your life demonstrates that you are living your vision.

CHAPTER 2

FUNDAMENTALS OF SUCCESS

On an episode of ESPN's Saturday College Football Final, football analyst Lou Holtz stated his four foundations of life, which were fundamental to your future and needed if you wanted to succeed in life. I found myself drawn to these foundations of life and agree with them. Mr. Holtz's four foundations of a successful life are:

1. To have something to do,
2. To have something to believe in,
3. To have someone to love, and
4. To have something to hope for.

I believe this list wouldn't be complete for me without adding one more foundation for a successful life that I have found to be important:

5. Plan ahead

These foundations were so basic, yet so profound and have enhanced my way of thinking, so that I believe everyone can learn something from them to build on successes in your own life.

As Tony Robbins has said,
*"Model someone who is already successful
because Success Leaves Clues."*

Having something to do is the reason we all wake up in every morning. I have spent over 35 years working and 22 years coaching athletics while raising a family. My point is that I am used to being very organized, busy, productive, and extremely active. These are the parts of my life that get me out of bed every morning. As blessed as I have been, unfortunately I have been put in several difficult positions where I was sidelined from all my obligations and activities. These events challenged my own foundations for a successful life.

Five years ago I shattered both of my femurs and I was bed ridden for over four months. I couldn't work, coach, exercise or be active. The worst part wasn't the sleepless nights or the chronic pain. After about two weeks I could tell I was getting edgy and frustrated and this was confirmed by my wife.

Without something to do, I would wake up in the morning not excited about life or anything that awaited me that day. My life wasn't fulfilling anymore, despite knowing that I have so much to be grateful for, deep inside there was a feeling that something was missing in my life.

One of the things that kept me going after breaking my neck was having something constructive to on a daily basis. Having something to do helps keep your life full of purpose, hope and satisfaction. It has been my personal experience that when I wake up each morning with a clear plan of what I want to achieve, I find myself focused and looking forward to what the day has to bring. I suggest you get in the habit of making a list today of the things you want to accomplish tomorrow so you know the minute you get out of bed what your goals are for the day.

In my book UP: *Getting Up is the Key to Life*, I detail the many "somethings" I did every day. My life from Monday to Friday started at 5AM with the alarm going off. I left my home at 6AM to travel to work. I got to work at 7AM and did not leave until 6PM, unless it was during football season. During football season, I got home earlier and went to practice for three hours. I spent most nights at the field where my sons played football and my daughter cheered. I served on the athletic board for years and coached basketball. I also committed to take my parents on a vacation every year, write a book, and create a successful relationship with God.

Having so many activities packed into every day helped me find purpose in life and renewed my commitment to myself and to the people around me. This made me truly happy. People who stay busy with meaningful tasks tend to be happier than those who are unproductive. Life without something to do is not living, it is existing, and you were not meant to just exist.

To find success in life, fill it with things to do that make a difference, and more importantly, have meaning to you. The possibilities are too numerous to count and the feeling that it gives you is infectious and empowering.

We all need to believe in something to feel fulfilled and successful in life. First, you need to believe in yourself, but it is human nature to want to believe in something bigger than us because it makes coping with life easier by putting things into perspective. This doesn't just mean believing in God, but believing in all things bigger than ourselves like coaching a team, working with a non-profit or raising a family. When our beliefs affect and involve others, our purpose in life grows. Believing in something gives us faith and hope. Without faith and hope what do we have? Part of the problem with the world today is that people are too afraid of stepping on someone else's toes to stand up for what they believe. Everybody believes in something, even if you are an agnostic or an atheist. For myself, one of my beliefs has been faith in Jesus Christ.

Every day we reveal our beliefs to the world through our actions. These beliefs can be seen through smaller actions like holding the door open for someone or saying thank you to grand gestures like running into a burning building to save someone's life. No matter what our actions, our true beliefs will shine through. Actions do speak louder than words, so the more positive the things we choose to believe in, the more positive our actions will be. Watch an athlete practice. Do they hustle or do they walk? Are they the first one or last one on the field? You might not know the contents of a person's mind, but we can know if their actions are consistent with what they say they believe. The most successful people in life live their beliefs daily.

Having someone to love is an amazing life changing feeling. People whom I love and who love me for who I am, make all the difference in my life. Love comes in so many different ways and forms and they all take you to an amazing emotional higher plane. The key to finding love is to get in the habit of giving love. As you give more love, you will attract more love into your life.

Here is the trick though, you have to first love yourself before you can truly give your love to others. As the love for yourself grows, so does your faith in yourself and others. As a father, I love my kids deeper than I could ever explain. I also have a passionate drive to provide for my family, and to position them for success in their own lives. As a husband, my love for my wife is indescribable. Showing your love to your family as well as to others brings you closer to God and helps you better understand His plan and it all starts with first loving yourself.

The love I have for the teams I coached or the professionals I managed is very different. It's not better or worse. This type of love has been a process of discovery throughout the years. This pursuit of my passion was a journey. Once you discover your passion, embrace it with both hands. Life is what you make of it and it is fuller with love in it. Don't let anyone tell you differently.

Hope is a Super Power

What is life without hope? Life is full of many obstacles, challenges, fear and disappointments. Hope allows people to approach these issues with a mindset suitable to success, thereby increasing the chances they will actually accomplish their goals.

Without hope, many times we become paralyzed by fear and we stop moving forward. When I was at home nursing two broken legs, life came crashing down on me. It was the second time in four years that I had broken both of my legs. I had gone from quadriplegic to an invalid confined to my bed with stabilizers on my legs that wouldn't allow me to get into my wheelchair. To make matters worse, I felt a cold coming on. My mind was overwhelmed with questions about my kids, my finances and my life. It began to strangle me until I couldn't breathe with the enormity of it all.

The disturbing part wasn't that these things were happening; it was that I had this innate sense that it would never get any better and that I would be stuck in this quicksand of despair, clawing for a glimpse of life forever. Hope opens the door to remind you of what is probable and opens the paths to the impossible. It was at that moment that I knew the value of hope. If you find yourself overwhelmed as I did, hope is the first step out of that deep, dark hole.

Many of us live our daily lives though the mindset and drudgery of "the way things are." Hope is the belief in what could be. If you have been struggling with finances, do you have hope that you can work it out? Do you have hope that your body can be healed from the illness that has plagued you? Do you have hope that the situation in your family cannot just be tolerable but good? Do you hope for God to do amazing things in your kids' lives? I do.

Sometimes what drives us daily or how we define ourself is

by what we believe is possible or by our hopes. When a shit-storm hits like when I was lying in bed with five broken bones in my two legs I asked God to give me hope. I put the situations in His hands and asked Him for faith that He would take care of them.

I admit that there was a short period where I lacked faith and hope. By the end of my pity party I felt completely changed. The situations were the same. My physical body was still weak, but I had hope and once I had that, I was moving forward once again.

I am a C 5/ 6 quadriplegic and I have what I like to call, a doctorate degree in hoping. When you break your neck at 17, you spend most of your time hoping, dreaming and praying. Hope is desire and we all have hopes. There is nothing wrong with hoping, it's a gift that is not taught.

Thirty-nine years later I am not disappointed with the an-swers to my hopes and prayers. Married over 29 years with three kids, my life has been full of disappointments which, as my father says, 'BUILDS CHARACTER". It is this character that fuels hope that keeps you moving forward to success. If you find yourself without hope in any area of your life, don't linger there. Put your hope in God.

Stepping Stones to Success

We have all heard, when you fail to plan, plan to fail. It is amazing how people who consistently succeed tend to have goals and self-discipline and then some. Basically, success comes with a price, but most things worthwhile do.

Winning and success are products of a strong vision, strong foundation goals, faith, planning, and preparation. I can tell you with 100% certainty that there is a price you pay for winning or putting yourself in a position to win. Part of the price you pay comes in the form of sacrifice, blood, sweat, and tears. However, without preparation, success will not follow. When success is knocking on your door, and it will, you need to be prepared to answer that door.

Part of being prepared may consist of warm ups in athletics or practicing a speech in business. These physical and mental preparations will give you a better chance to be successful in the real moment. No matter what sport you play or business you are involved in, you know that your state of mind before and during your game, business meeting, etc., controls how you perform. A calm mind will allow you to control yourself, which will result in a better opportunity to succeed. As a player, you need to be able to visualize your next shot, your next move or your next decision before they happen and believe that you can achieve it. Otherwise self-doubt will plague you and failure will prevail.

We all set goals, and if you don't, you need to start because your level of success will increase exponentially when you do. The one thing you must do to make your goals more tangible is to write them down. Seeing these goals every day will help to keep them in the front of your mind and make it more difficult to ignore. Hopefully by doing this, the actions that you need to perform to achieve your goals will become part of your daily routine. This in turn will make attaining your goals more accessible.

As Ralph Waldo Emerson said:
"Once you make a decision,
The universe conspires to make it happen."

Even when we create goals, write them down and perform tasks every day to ensure that they are realized, reaching a goal can still feel like a daunting task. One way to make this undertaking a bit more manageable is to take your goal and break it into smaller, more realistic, attainable goals. If you are a football coach, your goal is to win a championship. In order to win a championship your team has to be proficient in all aspects of the game, including your offense, defense and special teams. You can break apart what your team does at practice each day into smaller units. Coaches don't start creating a perfect offense by working with the entire group all the time, they break up the players into groups according to their positions. One coach can work with the linemen, one with the receivers, one with the quarterbacks, and one with the running backs. Each group has goals that they reach every day to make the offense better. This will eventually make the team better and able to accomplish their ultimate goal of winning a championship.

This same process applies to everyone no matter what profession you are in or position you hold. If you are an investor, your goal is to make millions of dollars. Your components would be stocks, bonds, mutual funds, precious metals and real estate. Each one of these diversified groups would be a part of your portfolio. If you are an entrepreneur, your goal is to build a million-dollar business. Your components are your sales plan, benchmarks, quotas and marketing process.

As a coach, I ignored my goal to win a championship and focused on the many parts of my team and what my team accomplished at practice each day. As a business leader, with so many elements to focus on and recognizing that each one was equally important, I always tried to remember that it was about the people, not just the recognition and commission at the end of the year. I have been blessed to be successful in both coaching and business using this method.

Winning a championship or being successful in life is a by-product of great preparation and excellent execution. If one component fails it causes strain on all the other parts and can cause total failure. I would be remiss if I did not reiterate that your best asset and most valuable resource are the people you serve. So, when you are preparing your team, building your business, or raising a family, keep this critical fact in mind. By doing so, you will increase your success rate exponentially.

So, if you wish to live a successful, happy and fulfilled life, ask yourself these four questions. Do you have something to do, something to believe in, someone to love and something to hope for? If you are not satisfied with your answers, change your situation. Find a way- Make a way!

Self-Reflection

1. What is your *something to do* that inspires you?

2. What do you believe in?

3. Who do you love?

4. What are you hoping for?

5. What are your goals for the next 12 months?

CHAPTER 3

POWER OF ONE

Everyone has the ability to be successful and control their own destiny. However, before you can accomplish controlling your destiny and being successful, you must learn to master and control one person. Look in the mirror and be honest with that one person. As I mentioned previously, master and control that one person looking back at you and you are on your way.

Reinventing yourself is a journey, not a destination. It is a lifetime event not a finish line. Reinventing yourself is a fantastic opportunity to make a better you. This could be a healthier or more athletic you. It could mean a more accountable and punctual you. There are no limitations to how or what you can reinvent yourself into.

Many of us, due to our age or our stubbornness, are set in our ways. Because of this, the process of reinventing ourselves is one that will take some time. This is when we have to think about and truly embrace the words of Lao Tzu about journeys of a thousand miles starting with one step. We have to retrain our minds to not only think but to know that changes can be made. When this is accomplished, our actions follow our thoughts and we begin to change our behavior. In time, these new behaviors will become so ingrained in you that they will be your own good habits.

In order for you to reach your full potential, you have to be willing and able to endure and pay the price. A coach, teacher, manager or parent would expect the same high level of drive and commitment. Are you willing to endure the pain and suffering it takes to be a champion? Anyone who sets their sights on greatness, whether that be in school, athletics, business, or life, will commit and push themselves to a high level. This willingness to push yourself is what separates successful people from the rest of the crowd.

The expectations would be for you to work hard, study hard, exercise hard, and practice hard. These are the things you need to do to excel and succeed. As a football coach at a smaller school, I had to compensate for having a low number of players on my team. When I started coaching at the junior high and high school levels, most schools would field a team of approximately 30 to 50 players. The school where I coached could only field teams with 18 to 22 players. Most of my players had to play both offense and defense.

I had to find a way to give my teams an edge. If I could help inspire them to embrace the "power of one" and value the extra effort and attention that goes into creating great results, I could compete with any team out there.

The power of one is evident in a simple scientific explanation. In the book *The Extra Degree* by Sam Parker and Mac Anderson, the impact of the power of one is made so easy to understand in the example of an extra degree. "The simple concept is this: At 211° water is hot. At 212°, it boils. And with boiling water, comes steam. Steam can power a locomotive. The one extra degree makes the difference."

This simple analogy reflects the ultimate definition of ordinary to extraordinary because it's the one extra degree of effort, belief, and faith in business and life that can separate the good from the great. This extra degree can inspire and motivate you or your team to the next level of success and beyond.

By taking ownership of this fundamental principle, focusing on a clearly defined goal, maintaining an unstoppable attitude, committing to take action, and persevering, you will witness life-altering, positive results.

As you get older you find out that life is a game of inches, much like football. Because in either game, the margin for success or failure is so small that you can never afford to veer off the right path. If a receiver is one half second too slow or too fast they don't catch the ball. The inches we need are everywhere around us. We gain that momentum to move forward and get that inch through our extra effort. In any struggle, it is the person who is willing to sacrifice and ignore the fear and pain who is going to win that extra inch.

In business, sports or your life you earn every inch. You claw, fight and scrape for that one-inch. Because we know when you add up all those inches, that is going to make the difference between winning and losing, between success and failure!

Throughout my coaching and professional career, I learned you had to play with the hand you were dealt. In sports, some years I had very talented athletes and some years the talent was average. It was the same in business. Some years I had very talented sales professionals and other years my sales team was average.

I was an average student, an average athlete and as I got older I knew I did not want to be average any longer. While watching a football game from the sidelines I heard a coach say "and then some" to one of his players and it stuck with me. After watching the game and listening to his explanation on the sidelines, he was talking about giving more. This statement resonated with me on and off the field.

"And then some" means if you want more out of anything, athletics, your job, your life, you have to do more than what is expected… and then some. Be thoughtful and considerate of others… and then some. Meet your obligations and responsibilities fairly and squarely…and then some. Be a good friend to your friends… and then some. Be the one that can be counted on in an emergency…and then some. And so, it is when we do what is expected of us in our lives and in the church…and then some; the Lord pays in full…and then some.

I started to implement the "and then some" philosophy into everything I did. As a wheelchair athlete, I did the same drills as everyone else and then some. I swam the same laps and then some. In business, I worked as hard as the hardest worker and then some. As a coach, I had my team work as hard as I have ever seen a team driven and then some.

Being successful is not just about working hard and then some. It is also about working smart. Have you heard the saying practice makes perfect? It is not true. Perfect practice makes perfect. Don't just work hard, work smart. Don't just practice or play hard, practice and play smart.

Seeing yourself as confident and empowered to be the best you can be is critical to your well-being, success and ability to be the one person that matters and that one person that can make a difference. We cannot allow ourselves to be distracted by thinking that the actions of everyone around us is driven by something we did or said. We could think that a boss, coach or person showing us little interest may not like us which could allow us to feel upset or rejected. This can turn empowerment into self-doubt. We may perceive events in a distorted way. In reality, it is more likely that they were busy or have a lot on their mind or any number of different things.

Remaining positive during trying times is not always easy as we have conditioned ourselves to think in ways that are not always productive. However, by taking control, by empowering yourself to think more positively, by creating that new habit, you won't fall into the stinking thinking, the not believing in yourself or your abilities trap.

I have learned that you can re-create yourself and be your best as often as you like. Being a quadriplegic, I have re-created myself numerous times. I am not going to settle and just survive, I am going to thrive! This empowers me to regain my confidence. With each new re-creation, I am more confident of success with the next.

In these uncertain, confusing and often depressing times, up again / down again economy, the world at war, corporate lay-offs, out sourcing and downsizing, what is needed more than ever is a personal pep-talk and reaffirming of how important you really are. No matter where you are on your journey to wellness, it is important that you build your resiliency by believing in yourself, thinking positive and empowering thoughts through-out your day that encourage you to be the best you can be.

Self-Reflection

1. Name one thing you can start to do in your life that could have a positive impact.

2. List one thing you can do to help re-create yourself.

CHAPTER 4

WISDOM VS. KNOWLEDGE

"We are drowning in information,
but starved for wisdom."

E. O. Wilson

When I was younger and had to write a report for school, there was a long, tedious process of information gathering that had to take place in order to accumulate the knowledge needed to complete the assignment. I had to go to the library, look through encyclopedias, read old newspapers on microfiche, and check out books. Depending on the subject matter, this process could take days or weeks. Nowadays any person who has access to the internet and can type or say the word "Google" can gather the same knowledge in a matter of minutes. With such a barrage of information just waiting for us to gobble it up with the next click of our mouse, our knowledge base grows exponentially every day. We now feel we can be experts on any topic from brain surgery to dog training. But having a horse does not make you a cowboy.

Having all of this information at our fingertips can fool us into thinking that we are more knowledgeable than we really are. Are we using all of this knowledge to be better people, make smarter decisions or lead better lives? This misconception can also lead us to believe that we are more entitled, have feelings of loftiness, and think that our opinion has more value than others.

Another common misperception that technology has given users is that they are smart or even worse, that they are wise. Don't fool yourself. Knowledge does not equal wisdom. Albert Einstein said, "Wisdom is not a product of schooling but of the lifelong attempt to acquire it." Even though knowledge and wisdom are similar, their differences are much greater. As a father, I have reminded my teenage son countless times not to mistake knowledge for wisdom.

In order for you to turn knowledge into wisdom, you must understand the difference between the two. Most people have a hard time understanding the difference, which is why they have a hard time dealing with life and finding inner-peace. According to Dictionary.com, knowledge is, "acquaintance with facts, truths, or principles, as from study or investigation; general erudition." Wisdom is, "the quality or state of being wise; knowledge of what is true or right coupled with just judgment as to action; sagacity, discernment, or insight." Therefore, knowledge is facts and information learned through studying, while wisdom is the utilization of knowledge at a higher level.

How are you utilizing what you have learned? Are you making wise choices about your food, health, job, and relationships based on all of your experiences in life, not just some facts or trends spread through social media? Wisdom is not a search engine. You can't go to www.wisdom.com and expect instant wisdom to be bestowed upon you just because you frequent that website. No one can make you wise. There is no secret class or magic spell to achieve wisdom. Wisdom is a lifelong experience. Wisdom, like many things in life, is a journey, not a destination. Wisdom is earned and accumulated like a savings account of knowledge over time. You must seek knowledge to awaken wisdom. The more we know, the more we realize how much we don't know. Every time you have an opportunity to make yourself better, you need to take advantage of it. You have that obligation to yourself.

It is extremely important to be knowledgeable in all subject matters, but that doesn't always help us choose the right path because facts can be swayed to fit any argument. Success does not make you wise. Titles of doctor, lawyer, professor or CEO do not make people wise. Those titles came from gaining knowledge, not necessarily wisdom. People who are experts in their field or who have received advanced degrees are too numerous to count while the truly wise are a much lower number.

The more you seek knowledge, the more opportunity to gain wisdom you will experience. Wisdom does not come with a label proclaiming itself to the world. Many times, we are surprised to discover it within us. It is like when you are talking and all of a sudden you pause and realize you have just said the exact words that your parents said to you while growing up and those words are relevant to the situation and exude wisdom.

We first hear wisdom from our parents and grandparents, then often from our teachers and coaches. We don't always recognize this as wisdom until we experience it, often times through a painful experience. Then as we grow, we recognize wisdom in life by example. Make time in your life to spend it with people who are wise and watch their examples. This doesn't mean just spending all of your time with older people. Although wisdom does grow with experience and that is why we often find it in older people, wisdom is found in people of all ages. Many young people have life experiences that have made them wise beyond their years. No matter how young or old these wise people are, seek them out and emulate their examples of wisdom. It will open up your mind to better navigate all that life puts in your path.

While listening to and following the examples of the wise people around you is an exceptional way to attain wisdom, you can also turn to other sources to find examples of wisdom to live by. One book in particular is the archetype of wisdom, The Holy Bible. The many stories and parables of wisdom in the bible can help us to understand how to take all of the knowledge we are privy to in this world and apply it to life's situations in the wisest ways possible. You can say it is the authority of wisdom.

Wisdom is a universal truth. Most people would agree on the basic fundamentals of wisdom, while knowledge can be easily debated. Wisdom is a positive that can eliminate many negatives. Many times in our lives we live with fear, doubt, uncertainty, and apprehension. These negative feelings and emotions prevent us from reaching our potential, our goals. Wisdom can unlock the barriers in our minds to allow us to approach life differently. Having a different outlook on life can help us to learn from life's lessons while deepening our wisdom.

A wise man never stops asking questions. Question yourself and answer honestly in order to truly understand your beliefs and your approach to life. Allow yourself to be open to wisdom growing within you, making it easier to deal with everyday situations. Don't get in your own way. There is so much more life to experience and each experience is an opportunity to gain more wisdom. Be practical in your wisdom and live by it without exception so that others can witness your wisdom and in turn become wiser themselves. I just wanted to conclude with a poem that I feel conveys the very clear definition of wisdom.

True Wisdom
By Michael Sage

True wisdom is not when we judge or ridicule one
another,
As none of us are better than one from the other.

True wisdom is not all the facts that you think you
know,
Every time you open your mouth for the entire world
to show.

True wisdom is not your version and the opinions
you convey,
But rather tolerance, acceptance and understanding is
the way.

True wisdom is usually conspicuous through silent
interaction,
And shown by the deeds that you continually put into
action!

Self-Reflection

1. List three (3) people you perceive to be wise.

2. List several of the character traits that they possess that cause you to perceive them as wise.

3. List three (3) ways you can improve your wisdom.

CHAPTER 5

POSITIVE CHOICES

Successful people, teams, and businesses have several things in common; they make good choices. Once you make a decision to move forward, like a tattoo, it can stick with you for the rest of your life.

Most of the problems you have are because of your bad choices, not what someone else has done. The solution to avoiding future problems is to make good choices today. Making good decisions is a fundamental life skill that, once learned, will benefit you for the rest of your life. Some decisions will be obvious and easy. They are the no-brainers and while other decisions will be harder to make, the principals for good decision making remain the same.

No matter what you learn and no matter how much experience you have, making tough choices is never easy. Down deep we all know the right path, the right decision, but many times we fall victim to not making the correct choice because it is too damn hard. However, it is wise to remember that you will keep getting the same challenges, facing the same choices until you figure it out and each time the situations will get tougher so, while making the right choice may seem hard today, letting it slide and having to face it again down the road will only make it harder.

The only thing worse than making a bad choice is making no choice. By choosing to do nothing, you are giving away your power and putting your future in the hands of someone else. You either take control of your life or someone else will.

You can have all the education in the world and still make bad choices. Good choices are a result of wisdom and being true to your heart. I have three children and one of the rules I set forth for them to follow was a very simple one to help them make good choices. This simple heartfelt rule works for any situation on the field, in an office, or just in life. Although the rule is simple and easy to understand, it is not always easy to follow. My rule is, *if you have to ask if what you are doing is right, assume it's wrong.* In our heart of hearts, we know when something is wrong. Occasionally we would like to ask or question our choice in hopes that we get a different answer than we already know. It is an internal struggle that we have all faced.

Choices have consequences, some are positive some are negative. The choices you will make in your lifetime may be complex, tough and have far reaching implications in your life. The wiser your choice is and the more due diligence used when making a decision, the better likelihood your choice will have a positive outcome.

With the advent of social media, it is more important than ever to make good choices because your bad choices could end up on the internet forever. The only way to realize positive change in your life is by making positive choices.

The principals required for making good decisions and leading a successful life remains the same as when your parents and grandparents were young. Learning how to make those decisions with wisdom is a skill that will serve you well for the rest of your life. While watching a video about Lou Holtz one day, he spoke about a set of principles he has to help make good choices. I thought that these principles were very practical and truly constructed a clear path to making good choices. His three principals were:

1. Do what's right and avoid what's wrong;
2. Do everything to the best of your ability;
3. Show people you care.

I believe if you follow these three principles, making good choices will become second nature to you.

You would think that doing what is right and avoiding what is wrong would be a no-brainer, but it can be difficult. Yes, sometimes trouble may find you, but we are talking about the times where your bad choices bring you to trouble. As for doing what is right, I believe we all have an internal voice that inherently tells us if it is a bad choice. The challenge is to learn to listen to that small voice inside all of us.

Doing everything to the best of your ability addresses an integrity issue. We have all had chores, practices, homework, and job duties. On certain days maybe you are tired, not motivated, or not feeling well, yet you make a choice to do your task. You finish it, but you gave it a half-hearted effort. That is not doing it to the best of your ability.

You made a bad choice. You chose not to give one hundred percent. Other times you had similar things to do and make similar choices yet despite being tired or not motivated you make the choice and superbly perform. Why is that? You made better choices. You chose to give one hundred percent. You chose to do the task or job like there was nothing wrong. You did the task the way it was meant to be done, the way we use to do tasks when our parents or teachers were watching.

Some choices we make may not seem like we are making conscious choices at all. Some of our habits and typical behaviors are choices. Habits are choices that we make so often that over time they require less conscious thought and therefore seem automatic. But they aren't. When it comes to bad habits, we may even be subconsciously justifying the bad choice automatically. We start to tell ourselves that the choice was made long ago and that we are now at the mercy of what has become automatic and we may even feel it is out of our control.

An example of this would be texting while driving. After years of texting while driving without an accident you may find it nearly impossible to stop texting while you drive. The sooner you take responsibility for your choices and acknowledge that texting while driving is not only dangerous for you but it is putting everyone else on the road in harm's way, the sooner you can stop doing it before an accident occurs.

You choose to text while driving. You choose to befriend people with good or bad habits. You choose to study for school. You choose to speed in your car. You choose to commute a long distance. You choose to get married. You choose to have children. You choose to be happy or crabby in the morning. You choose to let someone make you feel bad about yourself. You choose and choose. You have free will and choice so you choose your behaviors daily. You must accept ownership for the choices you do or do not make. Your freedom to choose is what makes you responsible for who you are. If you want to know whether or not the choices you are making in your life are good or not, just look around you. The people, the situations, the outcomes you see around you are an indicator and a reflection of the choices you have made. If you don't like what you see around you, it is time to make some new choices.

You realize that not making a choice is a choice. If you allow society to influence or relegate the raising of your children to emulate the role models of the day, that is a choice as well. We cannot have free will without owning our choices.

I believe that God desires for every person to make good choices, to choose wisely. Because it is my responsibility to provide for and protect my family, I made a choice long ago to continue to practice my Catholic faith and to teach these practices to my family. I used my free will to make this choice and in doing so, this positive choice has had a positive impact on my family. This doesn't mean that everything is always rosy. I still have to make choices every day to have integrity, treat others with respect, and to follow my core values so that my children can model this behavior and use it to make positive choices of their own both today and in the future when they have a family of their own.

What we become is a result of our choices. Most of us have made both good and bad choices. I will go out on a limb and say that most, if not all of us can say *but for the grace of God* my bad choice could have had a lifelong detrimental result. Those moments should have a deep everlasting impact on each of us. Remember the bad choices so that you can continue to make the good ones especially when they are hard to make.

As we all know, actions speak louder than words and "showing people you care" are the types of choices and actions you need to make. We have all been told by numerous people, "If you need anything just call," "Call me anytime for help" or ''I am here for you." We have heard it from family, friends, teachers, coaches, bosses and neighbors. I believe that most people say those words with the intent to actually help or be there because they want to be seen as caring people. Unfortunately, their actions or lack of actions scream, "I said I would help, but what I forgot to tell you is I would only help if it was convenient for me."

Showing people you care does not need to be a grand gesture. It can be something as small as a pat on the back, a note, or a nod of your head in recognition of someone's effort. However you want to show that care, be genuine with your words and actions. Make caring about others a choice you make every day and it will become a bona fide part of who you are and people will know that they can count on you.

One good choice leads to another good choice and so on and so on. Due to this repetitive pattern, it is extremely important to choose wisely all of the time, from the least significant event to the most critical life changing decisions we make because we never know how those choices are going to affect our lives or the lives of those around us. Even when we feel that life isn't giving us any options, we still have to choose. Start with the little things in life and build from there.

It may not always seem like we have a lot of choices, but we do, every day in small and large ways. With that in mind, I've made a short list of the choices we can all make every day:

- Choose to smile.
- Choose to be positive.
- Choose to be confident.
- Choose to live in hope, not fear.
- Choose to put yourself in the best situations possible.
- Choose to go outside of your comfort zone.
- Choose to forgive.
- Choose to live free of judgement.
- Choose to be strong.
- Choose to laugh.
- Choose to be happy.
- Choose to care for yourself and others.

My prayers are with you as you try to be all that God intends for you to be. I believe God is watching over you and me. God knows us personally. He knows what we're up against because He prepared our life's path. Like a mortal parent, God does not always intervene in our lives, or maybe he does and we don't see it or realize it. Either way, He lets us learn and make choices and He does give direct help to us through others. I believe he speaks to me through my mom. The most powerful assistance from God comes through our guardian angels that provide guidance and unmistakable assurance of God's love. I believe God has great expectations for us and expects us to grow.

Self-Reflection

1. Name three (3) positive choices you could add to your life immediately. Refer to the list above if you need ideas.

2. Is there an area of your life in which you have an opportunity to make better choices?

3. What can you do to help yourself make better choices?

CHAPTER 6

LEADERSHIP

The most dynamic leaders are made from hard work, persistence, attitude, faith and an undying passion. However, having the capacity to lead is not enough. A leader must earn the respect of those he wishes to lead and he must have the courage to be willing to use his leadership to gain it.

Author and motivational speaker John Maxwell often talks about leadership characteristics. When people make a decision to follow your leadership, they do it primarily because of several characteristics:

- They clearly see and understand your vision,
- They know you will create opportunity for them
- They believe in your skill set.
- They want someone to follow not someone to work for.

Leaders have dreams, are passionate and are willing to sacrifice. You need to dream in order to become a great leader. A leader who does not show his passion or share his dream will fail. It is important for any leader to remember that he must maintain close contact with the group if he is to function as a leader.

One of my dreams was not just to lead athletic teams, but to lead businesses, individuals, and my own family one day. My desire to serve, develop and create opportunity for others drove me to be a leader. I loved to help others see that their future could be brighter and that there were opportunities out there for them to embrace to create a better life for themselves. Helping people deal with negativity and self-doubt were some of the focal points of my leadership. I knew taking on any leadership opportunity would test my strengths and my weaknesses.

Leadership is a choice, not a title or rank. You are not promoted or born into a leader; leaders are created. I knew as a leader I would have to lead by example, pay the price and continue to grow my talents. I was the first on the field and the last one off the field. As a sales professional, I was the first one in the office and the last one to leave the office. In my home, I was the first one up in the morning and the last one to go to bed.

Showing this type of persistence and commitment would hopefully earn me trust, which is a key ingredient in any leadership role. It was my responsibility to help each individual find a way or make a way through the rough times. I had to show them the opportunities that existed beyond the obstacle because every time leaders are knocked down they keep getting up until they have overcome the obstacle.

Leaders find a way to get the job done no matter what happens. That is what makes them leaders. There are many strategies that leaders use to accomplish these tasks such as motivational speaking, leading by example, or finding the best person to get the job done. "Try not. Do. Or do not. There is no try." Leaders don't stop with just trying something or giving it a good effort because this usually ends in failure. Leaders are leaders because their efforts and commitment to success have been extraordinary and eventually end in success.

It is critical to do the right thing and get the job done correctly. I used to tell several sales professionals that worked for me, "Don't tell me how rough the waters are, just bring in the ship." It's easy to find people who will spend countless minutes or hours telling you how difficult something is to complete. They are the same people who will tell you how hard they tried and how much effort and time they put into a task without completing it. I don't know too many successful people that take comfort in hearing a long explanation on how or why something didn't get accomplished.

The characteristics and virtues of being a successful leader, like being disciplined, passionate, having a good attitude and a desire to grow, become a life style. You are either passionate and have desire on and off the field or you don't. You either lead by example in the office and out of the office or you don't. You don't turn these things off and on. They are a choice. You have to think it, speak it and live it, otherwise people see right through you. Perception is reality. If you are always positive and speak using confident, decisive words, people will see you as a leader and want to follow your example or be a part of your team. Once you start to think negatively and begin using pessimistic words like "I can't" or give excuses like "I would do that, but...," adverse behaviors will follow. People will see you as weak and will no longer want to follow your lead. If you want to know if you are an effective leader or not, just look at your team. Their attitude is a direct reflection of your leadership skills. If you don't like what you see, you now know where the problem lies.

As a sales professional, I was blessed with finishing in the top ten percent, three out of four years. I went on to help run the training department and was promoted to area sales manager. I was fortunate to have some great mentors. As a quadriplegic confined to a wheelchair, I had always worked inside. As time went on, I earned other opportunities, but I was never promoted into them. I knew there was a concern about the fact that I was never a premise or outside sales professional, but I knew I could develop, manage and lead premise sales professionals.

I had to ask for a new challenge because I could feel myself dying doing the same job after four out of five successful years. It was exhausting remaining in a job where I felt everything was just status quo. I went to the vice president of the company and told him to give me the worst performing outside premise sales team and if I did not finish in the top ten percent, I would resign.

I was promoted to take over the worst outside sales team in the company. I knew I would have to use all the leadership skills I had and improve my leadership abilities if I was going to be successful. I knew I would have to manage my time and multi-task more effectively. All my years of coaching taught me how to inspire and motivate, but I knew I was going to be tested since over half of my sales professionals were demoted from other positions within the company or they were new to the position.

I learned early on as a leader that the way you get what you want out of life is by helping others get what they want. Going to bat and being an advocate for your people is one of the most important things you can do as a leader to earn trust. Sometimes this is difficult because you must show your loyalty to your team or group even at the risk of displeasing superiors. Whenever a leader can create the feeling that each individual within that team or group is a part of the leadership and as they say, "has skin in the game," they hold themselves more accountable, making the team more successful.

When the people that you lead truly know that you care about them as a person, not just as an employee, athlete or student, they will understand that your motives for success are genuine and that you have their best interests at heart along with your own. People want to feel that they are a part of something, that their opinions matter, that they are making a difference, that all of their hard work is benefiting the group and themselves and they want to feel appreciated for their contributions to the team. This can all be accomplished when effective leaders keep the morale high in the workplace. One way to do this is to recognize associates privately and publicly. Recognition doesn't always have to be an expensive perk or a grand gesture, it can be accomplished through a pat on the back, quick comments of "Great job!" or "Thank you for all of your hard work," or a short note expressing gratitude and appreciation. So much can be accomplished when everyone is on the same page and working towards the same goals. Great leadership ties this all together.

Exceptional leaders balance all aspects of their teams. Being a leader takes a lot of selfless acts. It can't just be about you; it has to be about each individual on the team as well as the team as a whole. A team can be looked at as an open hand, which is a very useful tool, with each finger representing a person with their own individual goals. A leader brings all the fingers together to form a fist, which is united and powerful. Sometimes leaders don't listen to what their people are saying because they are too busy talking. Remember the quote by Epictetus,

"We have two ears and one mouth
so that we can listen twice as much as we speak."

To be a great leader you not only have to be a great speaker, you have to be an even greater listener.

To finish my story from earlier, I did succeed in my new position. I took the worst premise sales professionals team in the company and finished the year with one of the top teams. More importantly I took a team of four demoted, bitter account managers, four new account representatives and three seasoned sales professionals and turned them into a confident, energetic, and successful sales team. Ten out of the eleven exceeded their sales objective. Out of those eleven sales professionals, six were promoted into training or sales management and two were promoted to a higher level. Creating a successful environment is not an easy task, and maintaining a successful group is daunting. I am proud to tell you that in my second year with a relatively new team, we exceeded our objectives as a team.

Self-Reflection

1. What areas of your leadership skills do you feel are growing?

2. What areas of your leadership skills do you feel are dying?

3. Ask at least three (3) people what they perceive to be your leadership strengths and weaknesses.

CHAPTER 7

BE SIGNIFICANT

The real path to success in this life is to become significant. Significant by definition refers to being important or having a special meaning. Being significant in life does not mean that you are important, but that what you do is important and has an impact on others. Being significant means leaving a job in a better place than when you started. It is not about making you great, but making other people great. It is about serving the needs of others.

We must make our life significant! This is not the typical way we are wired and definitely not the way society drives us to be. We are not taught to think about our eternal happiness. I believe we were born in order to get a physical body, make decisions on our own, and prove to God that we can live in a way that allows us to come back to Him.

In a conversation with Tim Tebo during an episode of ESPN Saturday College Football Final, Lou Holtz told Tim that, "The good Lord put eyes in the front of your head and not in the back so you can see where you are going and not where you have been. Focus on helping others get what they want and you will be significant." I believe that life is about WE and not ME and when you understand that distinction and actually live it, you will feel and you will be significant.

Part of your goals in life should be to enjoy the highest levels of health, energy, success, spirituality and fulfillment. This requires an amazing amount of character, commitment, integrity and grit. It requires a great attitude and powerful, positive thoughts daily. All this being said, unless you make an impact on others you will not be experiencing a fully significant life.

People are motivated by a variety of factors. Part of our job is to find what motivates us to change or to do something proactive and use it to optimize our potential. To borrow a military saying, "to be all you can be." In order for you to accomplish this, you must be disciplined in your approach to life. Being all you can be is one thing, being significant is another.

I have been blessed with many great accomplishments in numerous endeavors. I have a great wife, wonderful family, am financially blessed, faith driven and successful in business and in my careers. This being said, there is no better feeling than the one you get when you feel significant. The first time I recognized this feeling was when I was 22 years old.

One of my goals as a young man was to coach football at the grammar school I attended. The grammar school was four blocks from my home and they practiced at a field about six blocks from my home at a park that I had played at growing up. After watching them practice before the season started I introduced myself to the head coach and asked if he needed help coaching or running calisthenics.

Al was the head coach and he was very welcoming. I was so excited to show off my knowledge of football to the kids and other coaches. As time went on and I became more involved with the activities of coaching, I started to realize I did not know as much as I thought I did. This was very humbling.

When the season was over I realized I learned quite a bit about football, a lot about myself, and even more about coaching. It wasn't until the banquet where I read some of the thank you cards the kids and families wrote that I realized I had a bit of an impact on these young men and their families.

After the season was over, I saw many of the kids and their parents out in the neighborhood at a store or at a restaurant and we had a chance to talk. It was not until then that I realized the true impact I made that season, the significant affect I had on some of the young men.

I went into the season thinking of ME. However almost everything I did was about WE. WE - being a player and me, the offense and me, the coaches and me. I realized that the coaching I had done made me feel significant.

I had done so many things for me through the years, as we all do, and there is nothing wrong with doing those things. Actually, many of the things we do for ourselves are necessary such as working out, dressing well, going to church, reading a book, going out, etc. These things make us feel good; they give us confidence, and a sense of accomplishment. However, when you think about how good some of these activities make you feel, none of these things really make you feel significant. That down deep, hold your head up, I made a difference feeling.

Helping these kids grow as athletes, teammates, and as young men was significant. Watching their doubts and fears turn into confidence and courage was astounding. Teaching them how to win with honor and lose with dignity gave me a sense of what it feels like to be significant. Coaching, developing and leading these young men was one of the most rewarding things I have done.

Years later I was reminded of just how significant making a difference in a person's life could be when I was asked by a former player I coached in grammar and high school who was now 26 years old to be his best man at his wedding. I was touched beyond words and felt honored.

One of the reasons I pursued the calling of coaching was so I could be and make a significant difference in people's lives. Being significant and showing people that they matter is the secret to success for every coach and business. I can't say it enough, you get what you want out of life by helping other get what they want out of life.

It doesn't matter what or who you coach or what business you are in or what product you have to offer. It comes down to what do your clients, players, workers and associates think and feel about you. The teams, groups, companies and relationships that fail over time consistently forgot about the people involved. Lose sight of people and relationships, and you lose sight of being significant.

The impact that a person can have on others is mind-blowing. We have all had a person in our life that has brought us up when we were down, shown us the right path to take, comforted us in our time of need, or made us feel like we were the most important person in the world. This person was different for all of us and held many different titles, but the outcome was the same. Through them being significant, they were a positive influence in our lives and we are changed, better people because of them.

It is your time to be that significant person for someone else. You have it in you, but the key is making it a part of your everyday life. Make it be the person you are. No one wakes up and says, "Today I will be significant." On the contrary, we usually get up and fall into the same routine we have every day. This is why it is so important to embrace significance because you never know when someone is going to take your words or actions to heart and change their life. You want that change to be for the better, not the worse. So always be encouraging, always be guiding, always be comforting and always be uplifting. If it makes it easier for you, look at being significant as a selfish thing. Never forget that you get what you want by helping others get what they want and by doing so you will achieve more than you ever thought possible and feed off an overpowering feeling of satisfaction and happiness deep within you. Your actions and service affect many people around you, both directly and indirectly. What you do counts.

Be honest with yourself when you look at what you have in life. I believe you will see that you have more than you thought. Consequently, if you look at what you don't have in life you will never have enough or have what others have. The most significant things I have done are adopt and raise three children, coach children and young adults, peer council people with spinal cord injuries, mentor young professionals, and donate time to charities, several athletic organizations, and my church. Building significance in your life is not always easy, but many times it can be accomplished by attaching it to a purpose. I know that God has a purpose for my life which allows me to build in my significance for not only myself and others, but for Him.

Achieving more than you ever dreamed possible may appear to be success however, there is more than just being successful required if you want to create a fulfilling life. Actually, being significant in life is more important than success. Not all successful people are happy while significant people usually find joy in their life. You cannot equate success to significance. People who brag about their success tend to have low self-esteem and lack significance. They find themselves focusing on the material things in life that leave you empty and lack real value. This does not mean that you cannot be significant if you are rich because one has nothing to do with the other.

Success is such an ambiguous term because it means something different to each one of us. Even though most people would get caught up with thinking having millions of dollars would make us successful, but they would be wrong. I am a C6 quadriplegic confined to a wheelchair and all the money in the world won't change my circumstance. Millions of dollars will not bring back our loved ones. The perception that money makes us happy is an illusion. Don't get me wrong, money can make life more comfortable, but comfort is often short lived.

Significance is the feeling that you matter and have a purpose in this world. It's knowing that you make a difference and you feel relevant, respected, and valued for who you are. As time moves on, being remembered by the people I had a significant impact on was one of the most rewarding experiences I have ever felt.

Success is sometimes a result of being significant but it is no guarantee, so don't focus on being successful first, instead, focus on being significant first. The happiest, significant people don't necessarily have the best of everything; they just make the best of everything they have. The following poem explains the importance of being significant.

Be The Best of Whatever You Are Be Significant!

"If you can't be a tree at the top of the hill
be a shrub in the valley but be,

The best little tree on the side of the hill,
be a bush if you can't be a tree!

We can't all be captains some have to be crew,
there is plenty of work for us here.

There is big work to do and lesser work to do,
and the work for US to do is near.

If you can't be a highway then just be a trail,
if you can't be the sun be a star.

It isn't by size that you win or you fail,
be the best of whatever you are!"

Author Unknown

Self-Reflection

1. On a scale of one to ten, how significant are you?

2. What can you do to be more significant this year?

3. Name three significant things that people do that you admire.

CHAPTER 8

EMOTIONS

I don't think you can find a more emotional calling than coaching athletics, football in particular. The highs and lows you mentally, emotionally, physically and spiritually deal with as a coach can be devastating, but the payoff for your effort is more than glorious. Coaching may be one of the most fulfilling and significant endeavors I have had the pleasure to be a part of. It is also one of the most challenging. The emotional roller coaster you are on is exciting, exhilarating and frightening until you learn to control your emotions.

What drives us to do the things we do in our lives? There are numerous answers to that questions like money, better opportunity, necessity, perks, or maybe it is because it is something we always wanted to do. These are all motivational factors that have an impact on us deciding which directions to follow in life, but one of the most impactful decision makers we have is our emotions.

Many times people need external motivation to accomplish the goals that they have set for themselves. Finding something that motivates us is an excellent way of reaching personal benchmarks on our way to attaining a long-term goal. The only problem with this is that many times external motivators lose their luster and don't have the same impact on us as they did when they first occurred. All of us have listened to a speaker, read a book, seen a commercial, or listened to a friend tell us a great idea and have been all gung ho to go out and conquer the world. Fast forward a couple of days and the excuses start to accumulate and we no longer have that motivation to accomplish our goal. One of the aspects missing on our quest is emotion. Attach an emotion to that external motivation and it can be a game changer.

Our emotions are deep within us and will never leave us. When the list of excuses starts to mount and we want to blame everyone and everything besides ourselves for our shortcomings, what we are really lacking is passion. We all know the things we should be doing, but that isn't enough. Tap into your emotions and let passion drive you to accomplish anything.

Emotions are a great asset that we have within us, but they are not always positive. That is why we have to control them. According to Elisabeth Kubler-Ross, "There are only two emotions in the universe...love and fear." While the highs are rapturous, the lows can be devastating both psychologically and physically. Continuously experiencing negative emotions can send us on a downward spiral that can lead to depressions, self-harm, or at the lowest end of the spectrum, death. On a more average, daily basis, negative emotions can cause us to have physical reactions and effect our behavior and our ability to function. Fear can trigger anxiety and cause us to break out in hives, vomit, perform poorly on a test, have headaches, and paralyze us where we stand. It also makes us turn down opportunities by making us question our abilities and decaying our confidence. You have to balance the good with the bad in order to maintain control.

I believe you can take negative emotions and turn them into powerful motivators. Much of my life I was driven by the emotion of fear. It's not that I lived in fear, but the fearful emotion of failure plagued me in many ways. The fear of not making a play drove me to practice harder. The fear of not being successful in business drove me to read, study and execute better than other professionals.

Emotions can affect us at any age and at any time in our lives. My reality at seventeen was staring up at the sky waiting for an ambulance to come. I will never forget the words that later came out of the doctor's mouth, "You broke your neck and you will never walk again." At 17, I was paralyzed from my neck down from a hit I took playing football the day after Christmas.

My emotions were going back and forth like a ping pong ball. At times I didn't know what to think. Little by little the fear set in. It wasn't that I had my life planned at 17, but I thought I was unbreakable. I had a girlfriend, I was working, going to school and playing sports. I was independent with a great family and blessed with many friends. All of a sudden, I could not move anything or control any of my bodily functions.

While my neck was throbbing like a toothache, I stayed awake one night watching and listening to a fly buzz around my face. I could not swat it. I lay there listening to all of the negative thoughts that flooded my mind. I was thinking of all the things I could never do or have. *"I can't walk or feed myself. I can't play sports again. I can't"*- BZZZZZ there was the annoying fly buzzing around my ears.

My mind went back to playing the broken record of life experiences that I would never be able to enjoy. *"I can't ever water ski, ride a horse, snowmobile, climb a tree, jump into a lake, ride a bike, drive a car, run down the street, throw a football or play basketball. I will never be able to go hunting or fishing with my dad"*- BZZZZZ there was the fly buzzing and landing on my head.

The thoughts continued. *"I will never get married. I will never have kids. I won't go to college. I won't be able to help my mom and dad. It is getting difficult to breath. I can't feed myself. I can't go to the bathroom by myself. Will this pain ever end?"* -

BZZZZZ there was the fly.

As the sun came up I realized the annoying fly was a great distraction from the negative quicksand my mind was sinking into. The fear was consuming me and there was nothing I could do. I swear I could hear my grandmother's voice telling me, "Say your prayers B," and I did. I woke up ready to attack the day and I turned my fear into motivation and determination. As time went on I worked hard at turning my negative emotions into positive actions.

The fear of being in a wheelchair and all the negative thoughts, feelings and emotions I was experiencing drove me like a run-away train. I needed to do therapy, exercise and gain back as much as I possibly could. I needed to finish school and get a great job. I needed to strengthen my faith and find ways to be productive. This interminable drive kept my negative thoughts channeled in a productive direction, for the most part. Unfortunately, the more I did, the more I realized there were so many other things I could not do.

Dealing with adversity is like jumping into water; you either sink or you swim. I choose to swim and it is not always easy. I look at adversity as a challenge, a speed bump. It slows you up a bit, but it does not have to stop you. Yes, sometimes it infuriated me, so I would go into my garage and hit my heavy bag until my arms were burning or my hands were sore. I found out that over time as I overcame the adversity and speed bumps, I gained more determination, and it inspired me to face every challenge knowing that when I overcame the adversity, I gained strength.

You have heard the saying *what doesn't kill you will make you stronger*. Well it is true. Adversity can change your perspective. I began to realize that my anger, fear, and adversity was just taking the negative thinking and transforming the panic and anxiety into action, into fuel for my soul. I discovered that I might not be able to have everything that I wanted in life, but who can? What came as an epiphany to me is that I could get most of the things I wanted in life, they would just be a little more difficult to attain and it may not be the same way everyone else achieved them. There is a reason that old sayings and idioms exist because they have held true throughout the ages. I was applying two of them to my life; *there is more than one way to skin a cat and happiness is not about having what you want it is about wanting what you have.*

This is one of my favorite prayers or sayings that I use to remind myself of the gifts and opportunities we are given that are often hidden in adversity.

The Creed for the Disabled

I asked God for Strength, that I might achieve.

I was made weak, that I might learn humbly to obey.

I asked for health, that I might do greater things.

I was given infirmity that I might do better things.

I asked for riches, that I might be happy.

I was given poverty, that I might be wise.

I asked for power, that I might have the praise of men.

I was given weakness, that I might feel the need of God.

I asked for all things, that I might enjoy life.

I was given life, that I might enjoy all things.

I got nothing I asked for but everything I had hoped for.

Almost despite myself, my unspoken prayers were answered.

I am, among men, most richly blessed!

Written by a Confederate soldier in the Civil War.

Every day we act on our emotions. The more powerful the emotion, the more dynamic our actions become. We all know that we should never let our emotions get the best of us, but I believe it would be safe to say that most of us have let this happen. I am not proud of it, but I must admit that when I was younger I had to patch a hole in my drywall as a direct result of not controlling my emotions. We have all been frustrated driving on the road and felt like cutting someone off or worse. We have all been angered to the point of wanting to break something. Thankfully most of these become passing thoughts and never become actions. Whether we became distracted by something else, our better sense took over or we took a deep breath and considered the consequences, we made the decision to act appropriately by controlling our emotions.

If you have ever played sports you definitely understand how emotions can and will explode on the field or court. When you are in the heat of the moment, you do not always think things through. Your position as a head coach, much like being a parent, puts you in the position of being accountable not only for yourself but for every person who makes up your team. This includes teaching them how to deal with their emotions while being involved in such a high-pressure game, on and off the field.

Acting on your emotions has consequences. Even though some situations can produce more intense emotions to deal with than others, remember that the only person who can make you feel a certain way is you. Find positive ways to release your emotions. If you are a physical person like me, get yourself a punching bag and hang it in your garage or basement. Then take time to keep hitting that punching bag, releasing your unwanted emotions. Otherwise the negative consequences can affect you now and maybe for the rest of your life. I can tell you with certainty that if you don't control your emotions someone or something else will.

As a young man, I was forced to deal with emotions and feelings that could take a lifetime to deal with. I was blessed to have an amazing family, friends and faith. I called it my trinity, which has gotten me through many difficult times and to this day I still rely on. My mom and dad were like the yin and yang of life. They were on opposite sides of the coin when it came to dealing with emotions. My mom was faith driven and had an unbreakable belief that she lived and imparted on those around her. My father was a very bottom line, get it done man. As long as you were smiling on the outside it did not matter if you were crying on the inside. I took the best of my parent's ways in learning about my emotional self.

Don't ignore your emotions or feelings. They are a normal part of our lives and need to be dealt with in a positive manner every day. When we ignore our emotions, they have a tendency to take over, which drains us of energy and wastes our time. This does not lead to a very productive and fulfilling life. Take responsibility for your emotions and actions, save your energy and go out and enjoy what life has to offer.

As a closing thought on emotions, I would like to tell you that playing or coaching football is the most emotional endeavor I ever was a part of, but it's not. Having a family and raising kids is the most emotional and significant thing I have ever done, but coaching is a close second.

Self-Reflection

1. On a scale of one to ten, how well do you control your emotions?

2. Name two areas of your life where it is difficult for you to control your emotions.

3. Name two things you can do to better control your emotions?

My first triathlon swim 1/4 of a mile.
Three months after shattering both femurs.

My boys keeping me company during a late night writing session.

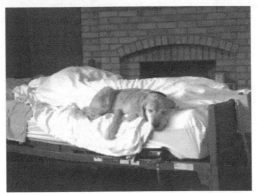

Einstein always knew when my shoulders hurt.
I finally got outside after 2 months of being in bed.
He would sneak up in bed when I turned.

Helping sponsor the triathlon.

Leading a Monday book club.

Teaching the young how to shoot and hunt.

Presenting a DAD, Disability Awareness Day, at a local high school.

Pool time for swim practice.

Taking the kids to the park for some practice.

Getting some exercise on the hand bike.

Helping others get outdoors.

Teaching my son how to use power tools.

First day on my hand cycle.

CHAPTER 9

UPS AND DOWNS AND DOWNS AND UPS AND DOWNS

We all have experienced ups and downs, highs and lows. While the ups can be thrilling and exhilarating, the downs can be devastating and crushing. I have been blessed to have experienced many ups in my life that I am truly thankful for. These uplifting events have woven their way through my life and caused numerous hours, days, months, even years by now, of joy and happiness that have made living delightful. One of the ups that I have experienced is becoming an author. Unfortunately, while riding the waves of elation that went along with two of my top moments of being an author, two catastrophic and heartbreaking events occurred in my life.

I spent most of 2013 trying to get my first book published. Countless hours were spent reading rejection letter after rejection letter, too numerous to count, until one day a small publisher out of Colorado finally saw value in my story and thought people would benefit from reading it and offered to publish my manuscript. I felt overwhelmed with feelings that ranged from being validated as an author and that what I wrote had meaning, to feeling a little giddy with a reassurance of myself, like when a girl would say yes to a first date. WOW! This was definitely an up in my life that I would remember forever and a high I will be riding for quite a while.

On September 26, 2013 my first book, *Up: Getting Up is the Key to Life*, was published and I was just waiting for it to be released. I was driving home and excited about the weekend and looking forward to the upcoming hunting season. I pulled up to the house and backed into the garage like I had done a thousand times. One shot and I was in the perfect position to open my doors and get out. I swiveled my captain's seat around and raised it up so I could transfer into my wheelchair. I slid the sliding board under my leg and slid over to my wheelchair. I rolled onto the ramp and lowered myself to the ground. As I was getting off the ramp, my wife Monica came out of the house and I stopped on the ramp to talk with her.

Instead of going up the ramp I decided to go outside. With my van doors open I could not go all the way down the ramp to get outside, so I cut off the side of the ramp, which I had done hundreds of times before. My wheelchair rolled forward and went off the side of the ramp. I leaned forward to push off the open side door to help turn. But this time, I started sliding out of the wheelchair. It was so slow! My butt slid forward and my knees hit the ground ever so gently. My legs got caught under my body and I fell back. I looked like someone stretching out their thighs. My 99-pound wife tried to grab me, and of course she couldn't. I just remember saying, *"Pull my legs out from under me! Pull my legs out from under me!"*

She could not pull my legs out from under me. I told her to run and get the neighbor boys to help. She kept asking, "Should I call an ambulance? Please let me call 911." I said *"NO, just get me in my wheelchair."* The neighbor boys finally came into the garage and I immediately asked them to pull my legs out from under me and they could. Once again, Monica asked, "Should I call an ambulance?" I kept saying *"NO, just get me in my wheelchair."*

I could feel my heart pounding. I had to stay calm. I thought if I could get into my wheelchair I would be fine. So, they got me in my wheelchair and I rolled inside and sat at the counter. Monica stood on the other side of the counter and asked if I wanted to go into the hospital and once again I said NO!

I lifted up my pant leg and looked at my legs up to my knees and they looked fine. I took deep breaths to help calm my racing heart. Monica stepped out of the room and I grabbed under my thigh to push my leg over and guess what? My thigh lifted up, but my leg did not move. I tried to control my breathing. I started to get light headed and tried to lift my other leg by putting my hand under my knee and lifting up. My bottom leg and knee lifted but my thigh just sagged.

Monica came over to me and asked if I felt hurt or if I was in pain. Honestly, I felt light headed, I was beginning to sweat and that meant my body was experiencing autonomic dysreflexia. This is a condition that some quadriplegics suffer from when some part of the body is in distress. If left untreated, it can lead to a stroke, seizure, or even death. My heart sank deep into my gut as it started to beat faster. Finally, I said to her "Maybe I will go into the hospital just to make sure everything is fine." She wanted to call an ambulance, but I insisted that I drive.

I started the van up, tore out of the garage, and headed to the emergency room. They brought me right into the back and got me onto a gurney and into a waiting room. I looked down at my legs and they looked fine! No bones had popped through the skin and there was no swelling. I actually felt relieved. I started thinking maybe I just tore a ligament or muscle. The doctor finally came in and by the look on his face, and the fact that I had started to have tremors, I could tell that the news was not going to be about a torn muscle.

The doctor said, "You shattered both of your femurs." The emergency room doctor explained that they could not operate and put pins in my femurs because my bones were too brittle from the lack of weight bearing exercise that had allowed a form of osteoporosis to develop. They could not cast my legs because they were worried about pressure sores and complications because I am a quadriplegic and could not do any pressure relief. In the end, they decided to just put soft stabilizer casts on my legs and keep me as immobilized as much as possible. I closed my eyes. All I heard was, *"You shattered both of your femurs."* *"You shattered both of your femurs."* Over and over.

I had just gone from being a quadriplegic to an invalid.

I was admitted and brought upstairs to a room where I told the nurse that the pain medication they gave me had no effect on the pain. The morphine they gave me did nothing. I was shaking, sweating and my heart rate kept rising as my body went into spastic convulsions. I closed my eyes, took deep breaths, and tried to slow my heart down.

The next day I talked with an orthopedic specialist who basically confirmed everything that the emergency room doctor had said. I was also told that it would be at least four months in a hospital bed healing, so I should start thinking of a rehabilitation or nursing home to stay in during that time. The thought of staying in a care facility scared the shit out of me. The possible complications I was going to face left me numb. After three days of excruciating pain they finally figured out pain medication that took the pain down to a level where I was not convulsing and shaking. The problem was I could not get this medication at home. To say my worries were overwhelming would be an understatement.

I talked to my family and we choose for me to come home and stay in a hospital bed in the family room. Even though there was a constant influx of family and friends stopping over, bringing meals and hanging out, my body felt beat and I must admit that despite all the support, I was unsure and down about everything. This was definitely going to test my strengths and my weaknesses. I felt like a pent-up cat lying in bed. I could hear the clock ticking. I kept asking myself, "How do I make the best out of this mess?"

After not sleeping for over 50 hours, you start to get physically, mentally, emotionally and spiritually numb. Even the sound of my phone ringing irked me. But one day, there was a call that would be worth taking. The phone call was to inform me that my book went to print and I better turn up my marketing efforts!!!

All of a sudden I was tasked with creating a book marketing plan, which included learning social media. I was not a technical guy. At this point, I still had a flip phone and had no idea what Facebook, Twitter, or any social media was. I had spent my life dealing with real people in a real world! This endeavor became the primary focus that would keep my mind busy, which was so necessary, at this point in my recovery. Now, my sleepless days and nights would be consumed by learning about social media and selling books! It was the beginning of my Facebook, LinkedIn, and social media life. I learned so much every day and I was excited to have my first book, *UP; Getting UP is the Key to Life,* published.

About six weeks into my rehabilitation, I started lifting weights in hopes of exhausting myself, so I could get into a decent routine where I was sleeping at night and not staying up 20 hours a day. The lack of sleep was starting to wear on me. It was around then that Monica noticed a rash breaking out on my back. It grew red, raw and irritated quickly, and since I had to primarily stay on my back there was no relief in sight. I remember thinking "God, shit keeps getting thrown at me to knock me down and I will keep on getting up with your help." Once again, I would go back to saying my prayers and thinking how I could make the best out of this mess.

About ten weeks into my rehabilitation I was having X-rays done on my femurs at home. Everything went well, and I was told they were healing well, but it would be at least another four weeks before I could start getting up into a wheelchair. Four more weeks strapped to this bed. This was going to be torture.

You can't imagine how many conversations I had with myself. Praying every day was a given, but the conversations that went on in my head were too numerous to recall. Even I was getting tired of telling myself that everything was going to work out! I had to keep my faith up. I had to remind myself of how far I had come. All the mornings I got out of bed no matter how hard it was. All the days I pushed on even when I thought I couldn't do it.

I wanted nothing more than to get back to my usual routine of getting up, going into work, coming home and exercising, running with the kids, doing projects, and staying busy. I had stopped coaching football, so I had more time to do other things like manage my health, write, get involved with a bible study group, and spend more time with my family. I worked anywhere from 20-30 hours a week, so that left me with time to manage other things. I enjoyed staying busy.

But around the 10 week mark, I had a day where I just wasn't feeling right. I could tell something was going on with my body. I was starting to sweat, my blood pressure was going up and I started to shake.

I had a feeling my catheter was blocked. My sister happened to stop in that afternoon and I asked her to get a catheter kit from the table so I could get the syringe and get the water out of the catheter, so I could remove it from my bladder. She texted Monica as she handed me the kit and I fumbled around trying to get the syringe attached to the catheter. We were able to pull the water out just as my body started to spasm and sweat profusely. I started to pull the catheter out. The pain intensified as my body convulsed. Monica walked in just as the blood started coming out along with the catheter. She rushed over with a towel and gloves to help and as she removed the rest of the catheter. A kidney stone the size of a bean came out, too. Even though I was a wet bloody mess, I had her take a new catheter and insert it back in. My body spasmed with pain as I urinated ten times the amount that most bladders hold. That kidney stone was preventing me from urinating! My body was going toxic. The pain dissipated over the next couple hours, but I felt like I just went 15 rounds with Rocky Balboa.

I remember trying to pray myself to sleep that night, but in the back of my head I could hear a voice asking, "What's next, what's next?"

By the end of the week, I was back to only feeling like shit instead of being dragged through hell. I just wanted to get back into my wheelchair and get back to my happy quad life. If only I could fast forward several weeks, I would be driving into work and back to my old daily routine. Believe me, I had a lot of work to catch up on and some of it I needed help with. Not only was I about a week away from starting to get in my wheelchair with bendable leg braces, but my new book was going to be arriving soon! I had been blessed with quite a few people pre-ordering them and those books were a bright spot in my life! To finally see it in print made all my hard work and publisher rejections worth it. Believe it or not, the work really started now, but this was a welcome distraction. It was time to create some public relations, marketing and sales relationships!

This also sparked a movement in me to press forward in other areas of my life. In an effort to push myself out of bed every day and to mentally give myself something to look forward to, I called the owner of a company that I had been helping out at since it opened. It had been in operation for five years. This gave me comfort, a sense of purpose, and a sense of accomplishment, since I helped with the successful startup and the successful five-year growth of this local company. The feeling of self-worth and being appreciated was wonderful. When I finally got in touch with the owner, my "spider senses" went off, as I called them. He kept it short and told me my services were no longer needed. No explanation. Have a nice day. Thank you very much. It was that quick.

WOW! Another kick to the groin!!

At this point, I felt like the bus was put in reverse and driven over me. And then put back into drive, just for good measure. Two shattered femurs, a burning rash, a huge kidney stone and all of that was still not enough to throw at the quad. Instead of succumbing to defeat, all this latest news did was piss me off. It taught me a lesson and lit a fire under my ass. I had a higher vision for myself! I had bigger plans with more meaning. I figured, God has his plans and I am not going to question or try to figure it out, I just needed to rise up again and move forward.

A key to rising up for me is replacing the feeling of depression with the feeling of being pissed off. Depression, at best, slows you down or drives you to a dead stop. Being pissed off is jet fuel for me. Think about it, would you rather be depressed or pissed off?

I knew there was something bigger for me out in the world. I had a grander vision for myself. I pushed myself even harder going forward. I finally got into a wheelchair and bent my legs so I could start driving, maybe a bit prematurely, but it worked out. All I had to do was endure more pain. And I did. I designed a web site, sold books, finished my nonprofit business plan and moved forward.

I could not have accomplished all of this without my faith, the grace of God, and fantastic support from my family and friends. Within four months of ''rising up'' again I started helping out at a different company with a group of men that would help expose my higher purpose and bring to the forefront a stronger relationship with God.

We are going to face many highs and lows in our lifetime,

very often on a daily basis. The key is to take the blow, deal with the pain, beat down the side effects, push through it, and move on. You may have to do this once a year, once a month, or once a day. The point is you can do it!

Don't listen to the naysayers because there will always be people around you that will be skeptical, ready and willing to tell you 50 reasons why something won't work. Don't listen to them. Listen to God. What is God telling you to do? Focus on that. Even when YOU become your own naysayer, tell yourself to shut up, too! Stay in a positive frame of mind, and always maintain a, find a way make a way attitude.

Self-Reflection

1. What process do you have in place for dealing with life when you are knocked down?

2. Name one thing that you do that is counterproductive to overcoming adversity. Describe how you can change it.

CHAPTER 10

PAYING THE PRICE

"You don't pay the price for success-you pay the price for failure. You enjoy the benefits of success."
Zig Ziglar.

We all realize that anything worth having comes with a price. There are no short cuts to success or accomplishments, just like there are no short cuts to becoming wealthy, losing weight, or doing anything worthwhile in life. Ultimately there are no free victories. Whether it is in life, business or athletics, your willingness to pay the price is essential to success. Some people set high expectations for themselves because they have paid the price through preparation, planning and execution.

Paying the price is a term we have all heard said by many people in different positions in life. I think of *paying the price* as I would think of making an investment in anything, the more you put in, the more you get out. The first time I heard it was from my father and mother most likely regarding school. I also heard it from so many coaches regarding making myself a better person and athlete and in doing so improving the team. The concept of paying the price also came up in my career from managers, presidents and different leaders. My understanding of paying the price truly grew when I coached high school football and reached its pinnacle when I became a father of three children and applied it to my life as a Christian man with leadership responsibilities to my family, workers, peers and most importantly to God.

I believe everybody pays a price in life but if you want to be more than average, if you want to make a real difference, be significant, reap the greatest return on your investment and be extraordinary, you will be willing to pay a greater price. The pain some people are willing to pay comes in the form of great self-sacrifice. They pay a higher emotional price; they pay a higher physical price by exerting a level of sacrifice and self-discipline that many are not willing to pay. Their desire to go from where they are to where they want to go is greater than the price they will pay.

Sometimes people are not willing to pay a high price until the pain of where they are is greater than the price they will pay to get where they want to be. There is a saying that *the difference between here and (t)here is the 't' which stands for time.* Without putting in a substantial amount of time, you would be like everyone else who tried doing something with a halfhearted effort and wound up failing. This leads to mediocrity, which is fine, if that is where you want to be. But don't expect that pain of where you are to dissipate unless you change your ways and put in that extra time and effort.

You have heard that you *can pay now or you can pay later.* When I was younger I did not pay the price for things I should have. That pain of regret I have lived with for years has been a very high price for me to pay. I now believe I should have paid the price back then. Like passing on a great investment tip only to discover that it quadrupled in price, the price you pay later whether it is in regret or lost opportunity definitely compounds and weighs heavy. Make the tough decision to pay now and invest in your dreams so you can reap the benefits of that choice for the rest of your life. Remember that Nike slogan, "Just Do

It!" Nobody said it was going to be easy, on the contrary it is quite difficult, but it will be worth it in the long run.

I come from a very blue collar, first generation college, "Johnny luck bucket" background. I also have the obstacles of not always achieving academically and breaking my neck at the age of 17 leaving me a quadriplegic confined to a wheelchair. If you consider yourself to be average, guess what? Average people can do above average or extraordinary things if they are willing to pay the price.

People want to accomplish extraordinary feats in life because the rewards you earn, whether that be financial, emotional, physical, or spiritual, are so much greater after accomplishing these exploits than after performing an average task. But in order to attain these grand rewards, the price you will pay and the investment you will be required to make in time, talent and commitment also become higher. Many times we see that the people who have these accomplishments are in leadership roles. It is a domino effect. Leaders may not always have been leaders, but they had a goal, stuck to their plan of accomplishing it, paid the price and reaped the benefits. This becomes part of who you are and after doing it time and again, people want to follow your lead.

Paying the price to achieve any objective comes in many forms and you must embrace these currencies and make them what drives you to move forward. You must be committed, be self-aware, and lead by example. Don't just say you are determined to do something, commit to it. When you are committed to something, you do it, not just make attempts and come up with excuses why something didn't quite work out. So, get up at 5 AM and actually go to the gym, get up on Sunday morning and actually go to church, or get to work 15 minutes early and actually make the extra five sales calls that you promised yourself you would do for the last six months. Your actions will mirror your commitment.

Being self-aware starts with being honest with yourself. Knowing your strengths and weaknesses are key. If you are willing to pay the price, don't put yourself into a situation that is impossible to escape with your current abilities. Don't use these as excuses, but set your goals accordingly. Otherwise this just leads to frustration. If you are only a high school senior you are not going to be a doctor tomorrow. However, you can plan for this through your course work in college and by performing well in classes so you can be on your way to the realization of your dream. Utilizing self-discipline in these situations is essential. No one likes to make sacrifices, but to see that light at the end of the tunnel, it is paramount to your success.

Leading by example is an excellent way to show yourself and others the price you are willing pay to accomplish a goal. We all know that talk is cheap and actions speak louder than words. Paying the price is all about taking action. When others around you see the steps you are taking to get the job done, they have a positive example to follow. These positive actions are contagious for both yourself and those around you making you want to push yourself even farther and showing others how they can grow personally and professionally. This also enhances your ability to be significant. This isn't something you learn from a book; we learn it from the examples set by others and practice it through old fashioned grit.

Everyone wants to be successful, but not everyone is willing to take the risk. It is like being down by on point in a football game with no time on the clock. Do you attempt a two-point conversion to win the game, or do you play it safe, kick the extra point to tie the game and send it into overtime? If you find yourself not willing to pay the price to be successful in an endeavor, then you have to find out why. Did you bite off more than you can chew? Are you managing your expectations? Are you just being lazy? Ask yourself these questions and be prepared for the honest answers. It helps to write your goals down to see where you can make some modifications. Seek out people that you know who have already paid the price and learn from their examples.

The greater your success, whether that is in sports, business, and even in your personal life, the larger and louder your critics will grow. Most likely you have experienced this in some facet of your life. While I was a sales manager in the advertising and marketing industry, I went through a long run of successful results. After my third successful year I could hear the negative rumblings amongst other managers and even some superiors. Do not let this negative talk create an obstacle for you trying your best and achieving your goals. Stay true to yourself. Remember, nobody takes a shot at the bottom. Stay focused on your own goals and keep moving forward.

Paying the price never gets any easier, as a matter of fact, it often becomes more difficult. But by doing so, you are putting yourself in a better position when opportunity knocks. All team sports have their starters and their back up players. There is no guarantee for athletes that they will ever be a starter. But for those who are willing to pay the price to keep themselves in the best shape possible, study game film, perform in practice as if they were starting and set the high standards for themselves, those are the individuals who will be ready to be a starter when the time comes. These players often become impact players on their teams and the type of player you can build a team around.

Your willingness to pay the price is one of the most important requirements for reaching a goal. Never put off an opportunity to prepare yourself to be better. Conditioning yourself to pay the price through commitment and hard work will increase your personal growth and open up your world to success. Get to the point in your life where you don't look at it as paying the price, but as just doing what has to be done. Because if you don't give it your all, there will be no one else to blame should you have to pay the ultimate price in the form of failure.

Self-Reflection

1. Think of two areas of your life where you can step up your game and pay the price.

2. Specifically describe the ways you could go the extra mile, make a larger investment in your dreams and pay the higher price in order to make them a reality.

CHAPTER 11

ATTITUDE

"Watch your thoughts; they become words. Watch your words; they become actions. Watch your actions; they become habit. Watch your habits; they become character. Watch your character; it becomes your destiny."
Lau Tzu

How do you want to face your day? Do you want to be happy or miserable? Upbeat or a downer? It doesn't matter if you got an A on a test in calculus, you gained six pounds after being on a diet for two weeks, you won the lottery, or God forbid, your dog died. You can choose what your attitude is going to be in each one of those situations. It isn't always an easy choice to make, but remember to choose wisely.

Your attitude can make you or break you, make you succeed or fail. It doesn't mean that you will be able to accomplish anything just because you have a great attitude, but choosing a negative attitude guarantees you will make it harder to succeed. If you find that you are deficient in talent, skills, knowledge, or experience, which impedes you from accomplishing a goal, it is much easier to ask for and receive help from others when ou approach a task with a positive attitude. Having a positive attitude doesn't make you a better person, but it does make you easier to be around.

Controlling your thoughts, which affect your attitude is critical. You can see the importance of controlling a person's thoughts, emotions and attitude in sports. You have seen coaches "ice" a kicker in football or someone shooting a free throw in basketball by calling a time out. My son was a quarterback, and when he threw an interception I used to tell him, "You need to have a short memory." I knew the longer he thought about it, the more likely his attitude would become less confident and less positive. Many athletes become less self-assured during these times, causing them to miss a field goal or free throw or throw another interception.

The most powerful tool that we possess is our mind. It is constantly sending subconscious messages to different parts of our body telling it how to function properly while millions of conscious thoughts run through it at the same time. Our mind is also a product of its environment causing it to think the same way other influential people around it think. If the people around us are confident thinkers with positive mental attitudes, this is an ideal situation and we learn to be optimistic people with outgoing personalities and awesome attitudes. The problem is that most of us don't think that way. Our minds are full of the worries that go along with everyday life trying to problem solve through the day. We focus on the one thing we did wrong instead of the numerous things we did right. We feel guilty when we don't have time to cook a great meal and attend an evening event after working a full-time job. All of these pessimistic thoughts flood our brains and have an adverse effect on our attitude. This is where training comes into place. Zig Ziglar addressed this topic when he said, "You are what you are and where you are because of what has gone into your mind. You can change what you are and where you are by changing what goes into your mind."

Training yourself to have a more positive attitude may не be a quick process, but can be accomplished. Use your favorite form of entertainment to learn different methods to form a more confident way of thinking. If you enjoy watching movies, watch upbeat movies with encouraging messages. If you love to read books, there are countless motivational stories and quotes that address this topic. If listening to music puts you in the right frame of mind, put your headphones on and listen to your favorite playlist. If you like to exercise, go to the gym or jog around the block. If you love to socialize, surround yourself with optimistic, confident, happy people. The transformation will astound you. If all else fails, spend a few minutes focusing on the many things you already have in your life to be grateful for.

We are constantly bombarded with situations we have to deal with every day. It is called life. We do not have any control over most of what happens in our lives. Even though this can be frustrating at times, it doesn't stop things from happening. The only thing we do have control over is how we react to what happens to us.

It is perfectly normal to experience a broad range of emotions that impact our attitude which in turn drives our actions and behaviors. When things are going well it is usually easy to have a positive attitude, but when things go wrong you have a choice to make. It may be fitting to be angry or frustrated in many situations, but how long do we stay angry, frustrated, depressed, irritable, or fuming?

Everyone needs to do what I call, "The Checkup from the Neck Up." Whether life is going good, bad or indifferent, you have to ask yourself; how do I want to feel? Do I want to feel better or feel bitter? How do I want to be perceived? Am I going to deal with this situation now or am I going to let it ruin my entire day? Using a positive attitude to deal with issues will increase your happiness and success. A positive attitude allows u to move on from a negative situation and go on with your ay. This enables you to either complete whatever task or project you were working on or begin other exciting endeavors. It allows you to have less worries and think more clearly. Life should not be something that you just get through, moving from one moment to the next waiting for the other shoe to drop. Take your upbeat attitude out for a spin. Your confident attitude will be visible to others through your body language and make you more approachable. Your positive attitude will likely spread to the people around you. People want to socialize with other people with positive attitudes because they smile more, laugh more, and are more fun to be around. The effects of your positive attitude will be a more powerful drug than you could ever take or chemical substance you could put into your body.

I had a vice president address my sales office with less than good news. When he heard people's response to the bad news he gave us advice. He said, "Instead of saying that sucks or worse, say that's interesting and try to figure out how to make it a better situation." I started using the word interesting and bad news became less devastating and easier to address and overcome.

We all know someone, maybe an athlete maybe a business person you work with that always seems to have things go well. They just excel and seem to be happier more often. You are probably thinking, they are happy and have great attitudes because things are going their way. Or are things going their way because their attitudes are good? It's the old chicken or the egg question. Well, I can tell you this. I have been around thousands of athletes and hundreds of business executives and without question, the great ones, the really successful ones, had fantastically positive attitudes.

Positive change may not happen overnight. It is a journey, not a destination. The journey is trying to maintain a positive attitude when you feel like you don't care, when you have been sick or you are being annoyed. With a positive attitude, you see the bright side of life, become optimistic, and expect the best to happen.

One of the biggest questions I get asked is how do you maintain a positive attitude when you are in a wheelchair? My response is that I have been blessed in so many ways. I have so many choices every day on how I will react to difficult or unfair situations and I choose to think positive about as many things as I can. While choosing a positive attitude doesn't always change things immediately, choosing a negative attitude will change things for the worse, make things even harder for you, almost immediately. I also thank God, for all the great things he has given me. As a coach, leader, father or just as a person I had to become a creative thinker. I did not want to ever let my wheelchair or any circumstances get in my way of moving forward, being successful and living a happy life.

Sometimes when we come in contact with or see confident, optimistic people on television or the internet, we assume that they are always happy and never have awful things happen to them or experience rough patches in their lives. This just isn't true. Successful, determined, confident people turn negatives into positives. Having a bad attitude never makes any situation better or changes the fact that it happened. Michael Jordan, one of the greatest basketball players ever to play the game, tells about how negative situations impacted his life and how he dealt with them. He said, "I've missed more than 9,000 shots in my career. I've lost almost 300 games. Twenty-six times I've been trusted to take the game winning shot… and missed. I have failed over and over and over again in my life. And that is why I succeed." He not only succeeded, he changed the mindset of his entire team, bringing the best out in each athlete and winning six NBA Championships with the Chicago Bulls. That's what I call being a significant leader by inspiring those around you by your own example.

If you currently don't possess a positive attitude and things e not looking too bright in your life, change your ways. The people who really want to accomplish things find a way to make it happen. They do not fall back on excuses and claim other people are just lucky. People have been falling into this bad habit for so long that there is an old saying about it, "If 'ifs' and 'buts' were candy and nuts, every day would be Christmas." People say, "I would have done that, but...." or "If I had more time I would ....". Don't let the "ifs" and "buts" get in your way of being the best you can be. A bad attitude is a disability.

Self-Reflection

1. On a scale of one to ten, how would you rate your attitude?

2. List three ways you can create and maintain a positive attitude.

3. What attitudes do you want to discontinue: greed... guilt...endless negativity?

CHAPTER 12

THE BEAT DOWN

God doesn't like to see us in pain, to stumble, or feel sad and depressed, but He knows that our experiences in life will refine us, or as my dad says, "It builds character." We can choose to make the best of the most trying circumstances, and we can become better because of them. God will be there to support us along the way. God's plan may sound easy, but as I have learned, life is full of both ups and downs.

Four years after my fist incident of being knocked down, I was headed out one night to meet with a group of people who were interested in having a fundraiser to benefit the 501 (C) (3) non-profit called (SOAR) Swift Outdoor Accessible Recreation that I had started in 2015. We were meeting at a restaurant about thirty minutes away from my home.

I hopped in my van and transferred over into the driver's seat and headed out to meet the motorcycle club that I had become friends with. It was Wednesday so I was not surprised to arrive to a relatively empty parking lot where I transferred back into my wheelchair and got out of my van.

I flung open the door to enter the building and twisted my wheelchair straight in the doorway. There was about a three-inch threshold to get over, but I had hopped over those numerous times. As I popped my front casters over the threshold and nged forward to get my back wheels over, my anti-tip bars caught the lip and stopped my wheelchair from rolling forward. My body slid forward as I tried to grab my wheels to stop myself from sliding forward to the ground. My knees barely touched the ground before a large man grabbed my arms. Another guy rushed over and they both lifted me back into my wheelchair. With my heart beating out of my chest, I brushed myself off and made a joke about what just happened.

I rolled over to a table where several guys were sitting and we had a discussion about the fundraiser for SOAR. One of the guys from the motorcycle club was a man I coached in football in high school. That was over twenty years ago, but I remembered it like it was yesterday. In high school, he was a receiver and his name is Mike. I remember meeting him and thinking, "Really? I have a receiver with four fingers and thinner than a straw?" We laugh about it now, because he used to think, "GREAT! How in the hell is this guy in a wheelchair going to teach me how to run routes and be a great receiver?" Mike was, and still is, a great athlete and an even better man.

On my way home I felt my knees and legs to see if I could feel anything wrong, but luckily they felt fine. When I got home I transferred into my wheelchair and went inside the house. I told Monica about my fall but didn't want her worried. Even though I felt fine, I slid into bed so she could check out my legs.

There was a bruise and a small bump on my one knee, but I was relieved to see that nothing looked out of place. You can't imagine the relief for both of us. That night I started to sweat and shake which is a sign for a quadriplegic that there is something wrong. I did learn something from the last time I hurt my legs, and that was that I was not going to drive myself into the hospital this time. With the condition I was in, I called an ambulance. After a quick ride to the hospital, we sat waiting for x-rays on my knee. As usual, the pain medication, which was morphine, had no effect on me. This was partially due to the fact that I am a quad and with my nerves severed, the medication can't tell the brain to stop sensing pain.

This time I really thought I had a pulled or torn a muscle or ligament, but the emergency room doctor set me straight. He came in and told us that I had broken both fibulas, both tibias and my one femur. He took Monica and my sister out of the room to look at the x-rays. When they came back into the room, Monica was in tears. My heart sank knowing what was ahead of us. The five days in the hospital were easy compared to the long healing process that would take place at home.

The last night in the hospital was a nightmare. The thought of what Monica would be put through, while working, sickened me. That, along with the stress and work it put on my kids, mom, dad and sisters dragged my thoughts into a very dark place. I just dreaded what was to come and there was no easy way to get through the next three to four months in a hospital bed in my family room.

How was I going to deal with this again? It felt so different from the first time I shattered my femurs. That feeling of being helpless and a burden was turning my stomach. I lay there thinking, "How much can the people around me take? How in the hell do I turn this black cloud into a silver lining is beyond me."

I was sent home in an ambulance after my stay in the hospital. Once again, we rented a hospital bed and put it in our family room. I was glad to be home, but I knew it was going to be a long painful road to recovery. The air mattress on the hospital bed was the most uncomfortable bed I had ever experienced. I had to lie on my back for the first two weeks.

My sleep patterns were so messed up I would only nod off for about two hours a day. I tried everything I could to exhaust myself, so I could sleep for more than two hours a day. I tried reading, writing, watching television and lifting weights, but nothing helped. Staying awake for 36 to 48 hours was not unusual.

Even though I was blessed with supportive people who would stop over, the feeling that I had to entertain them, be upbeat and engaging was grinding on me. At least I was slightly distracted from the constant sweating, shaking and shots in my stomach to prevent blood clots. I tried getting back to writing a book I had started, but I could not put two decent sentences together. My mind would go blank or go to a dark place where my heart would start pounding and my mind would be flooded with so many frustrating thoughts and questions.

Watching life go by was painful in so many ways. Even worse was watching the wear and tear it had on Monica and the family. Lying there helpless sucked and it was wearing on me. I tried not to be needy for attention during the nights when everyone was home, but the days alone while everyone was at work and school just dragged on.

I was really struggling mentally. I tried to take all my own positive advice and wisdom, but it wasn't having the positive impact I expected. I also knew that Monica had far less support than she did before. Both our mothers were dealing with other issues and our oldest son moved out, which we were happy to see him take that next step in life, but we missed him.

I finally was able to spend at least eight hours in my wheelchair wearing metal leg braces that went from my upper thigh to my calf. I was able to get out and ride, a needed relief and freedom I missed dearly. Becoming more active definitely helped calm my nerves a bit and I started to sleep a bit more regularly.

A month in my wheelchair and I felt like I was just coasting or getting by. I needed a spark or a bigger goal or something. I knew it might be too late to attempt this, but I signed myself and my three kids up for the Manteno sprint triathlon. They were young and could be ready with little preparation, however I did not have the same luxury as being young and active. I just spent four months in a hospital bed and only had three months to try to get in the water to train for the four-hundred-yard swim.

As you could imagine, this decision did not go over very well with my wife, my parents, and even several friends questioned my sanity. I must admit I had a little self-doubt about attempting this triathlon less than three months after having five broken bones in my two legs. "Go hard or go home," I had said countless times to others and now it was my back against the wall.

I tried to get to a lake, but I could not find any support to help me in and out. About two weeks later I was able to get in my sister's pool and get in some laps. As I suspected I had no endurance and my breathing was terrible evidenced by the fact that I kept taking water in through my nose. After that pathetic display even I had a little negative self-talk going on in my head.

I was only able to get into the lake once, which was two weeks before the triathlon. I was representing SOAR as a team. My youngest son, 15 years old was doing a 13-mile bike, my oldest son was doing the three-mile run and I was doing the 400-yard swim. I also entered my 17-year-old daughter to do the swim on another team. It was a great cause, all the money raised was going to a local veterans' home.

Never let them see you sweat and race day was here. I was trying not to think about the fact that three months ago I was lying in a hospital bed and I only truly got one practice swim in. So, I was dragged down to the water and they pulled my wheelchair in up to my lap and I flopped in. Not pretty, but effective.

I had another swimmer next to me, not by choice, to help me navigate since I was doing the back stroke. The whistle blew and I was off. In my head I kept saying, "if you can take it you can make it!" I just tried to get my breathing down into a good repetition with my arms. I tried to reach as far back as I could and grab as much water to pull myself through. I even imagined my feet kicking.

We hit the buoy, which was the half way mark, and I could

ear the other swimmers. On the swim back every time my arms got tired or it was difficult breathing, I kept thinking about laying in that hospital bed in pain. With every stroke I tried to put that memory of lying in bed for four months behind me. My arms struck the water pulling forward, there was no pain and I don't even remember breathing for minutes.

The next thing I remember was hearing voices from the beach, the finish line. I felt the sand hit my fingers and I finished to the sound of family and friends cheering me on. Wow it is amazing what your mind can do.

Riding my high from the triathlon carried me through the summer and into the fall. I was getting back into my routine and continuing to do the many things in life that I found rewarding. One of those things was writing this book. Before I finished, Einstein got sick. He was my seven-year-old service dog. An amazing golden retriever, you could not ask for a better friend, or a more loving, loyal, smart and caring dog than Einstein.

I got to wake up to his smile and wagging tail every morning. He sat in bed and would steady himself as I gave the command of HOLD, while I grabbed him to pull and turn myself over on my side. He was there to pick up anything that I dropped and would bring it right to my lap and hand it to me without a bite mark.

Monica and I spent hundreds of hours training him from a puppy using the commands taught and used in the training manual from My Angels with Paws. The training was intense and very specific, especially when it came to commands. There was a weekly lesson plan on how and what to train him. It was very time intensive, but the results were amazing.

Einstein could open and close the doors, get me the remote, or pull my phone out of my pouch when it was ringing. After I got up he sat patiently by the bone box waiting for a treat, no barking or haunting, just waiting for me to come and reward him.

At meal time with the command of GO IN he would go under the table and lay down with his head resting on my feet or foot-rest waiting for me to drop a morsel of food. We could all get up and walk away and there he would stay just looking up until we gave him the words GOOD GO IN. He would then sprint over to the bone box for a treat.

Several times when my shoulders or elbows were in severe chronic pain he would jump up on the bed and crawl up by my shoulder and neck and curl up around them as to warm them up, which was a great relief. This amazing service dog was frighteningly intuitive.

Einstein not only made my life a joy but also put a smile on my entire family's face. I swear he was better than any medication that could be prescribed especially for my teenage son. As a teen, my son had a problem with authority and hated school. As he went through his angry teen years there was only one thing that could help him, and even he did not realize it! My son could be in one of his angry "everyone sucks" moods or walk in from school pissed at a teacher, the school, or all of them at once and Einstein would still meet him with a smile and a wagging tail. Within 10 to 15 minutes, like magic, most of my son's anger and frustration were gone. Even my mother in law, who did not like dogs and was actually afraid of them, found a place in her heart for Einstein.

On October 26, 2017 we brought Einstein into the veterinarian for a bloody nose. Even though we were told it could have been from rough-housing with our son's puppy or from running through the bushes and trees, I had a bad feeling. I was noticing him feeling thin as I petted him and I noticed him struggling to stand. The following morning, we brought him into the vet for blood work and x-rays. The blood work showed he had cancer. It was probably some type of leukemia. The x-rays showed an enlarged liver, spleen and esophagus. He also had an extremely low red blood cell count, a high white cell count, and a fever.

My heart sank. I could barely catch my breath as I comforted Monica while she cried on my shoulder.

Over the next 48 hours his breathing became more strained and he vomited numerous times. Despite the fact that each time got worse and worse, not one cry or whimper came from him. When we talked to him he would wag his tail and only lift his eyes to see us. By the end of the day he could not stand and was drooling on the floor. I knew I could not let this amazing friend suffer.

On October 31st, my two youngest children, Monica and I brought him back to the vet to do the only humane thing. We had to get a cart from the vet to put him on as he was too big to carry, and he could not walk. With the three of them in tears, I struggled to hold mine back as I held Einstein's head in my hand. I rubbed him and prayed as we waited for the doctor. The doctor explained the process, which we already knew, and went to get the shot that would relieve his suffering.

My wife and kids cried and petted Einstein as I held his head. I had to close my eyes and take deep breaths to restrain myself from losing it. Sitting there, seeing my family in tears and holding my best friend's head left me feeling helpless and lonely. That feeling of despair welled up in me and I could not hold it in. I allowed the tears to run down my face and my nose start to drip.

The door opened and the doctor came in with the shot for Einstein. She went to his back leg and injected him. I removed his dog collar and name tag and gave it to my son to hold. We all stood there rubbing Einstein as he slowly fell asleep. I took his head that I was holding and rested it on the cart.

I said my final goodbyes, prayers and thanked him again for being an amazing friend as my kids and wife cried over him. I felt that I had to be strong for my family. I only allowed a few tears to roll down my face while my son cried on my shoulder and my wife cried in my arms. I have spent many years suffering in silence and this was no different. I was strong, once again, because I had to be. Our family could never have asked for a better friend.

Whether you feel blessed or cursed, whether you're in a wheelchair, poor, rich, talented or supremely average, you are expected to make the most of what you've got. I do believe there was a purpose to my pain. Although I do admit I have no idea what I am supposed to learn out of this with the exception of testing myself at a higher level. I took a lot of time to pray or to channel positive energy. No matter what you might face, try to look at the bright side of the situation and call on your angels or spirit guides for higher wisdom. Prayer will put things into perspective.

Being sentenced to that hospital bed and Einstein's death were two of the most difficult things I have ever experienced in my life, but I had to keep going. Remember, there will be circumstances you can't control or change, but you can always change your attitude and the way you deal with your circumstance. You need to learn how to dig a little deeper when you think you can't dig any more. I was able to implement this in life, business, sports, and my family. Getting UP and moving forward became the only way I know.

Self-Reflection

1. Name three (3) positive ways you can deal with loss.

2. Name something that you can do to end your day on an UP.

CHAPTER 13

MOVING FORWARD WITH PURPOSE

"What lies behind us and what lies before us are tiny matters compared to what lies within us."
Ralph Waldo Emerson

We all need purpose in our lives. We have to have accomplishments, even small ones, that keep us going. In a speech to the graduating class of 2014 at the University of Texas, Austin, naval Admiral William H. McRaven addressed the graduates about the importance of having small accomplishments lead to larger accomplishments. He said,

> "Every morning in basic SEAL training, my instructors, who at the time were all Vietnam veterans, would show up in my barracks room and the first thing they would inspect was your bed. If you did it right, the corners would be square, the covers pulled tight, the pillow centered just under the headboard and the extra blanket folded neatly at the foot of the rack — that's Navy talk for bed.
>
> It was a simple task — mundane at best. But every morning we were required to make our bed to perfection. It seemed a little ridiculous at the time,

particularly in light of the fact that were aspiring to be real warriors, tough battle-hardened SEALs, but the wisdom of this simple act has been proven to me many times over.

If you make your bed every morning you will have accomplished the first task of the day. It will give you a small sense of pride, and it will encourage you to do another task and another and another. By the end of the day, that one task completed will have turned into many tasks completed. Making your bed will also reinforce the fact that little things in life matter. If you can't do the little things right, you will never do the big things right.

And, if by chance you have a miserable day, you will come home to a bed that is made — that you made — and a made bed gives you encouragement that tomorrow will be better.

If you want to change the world, start off by making your bed."

After I got hurt, I had my father rig a set of weights for me to use so that I could do one thing every day to build up my strength and keep myself moving forward. I kept the weights next to my bed. There were mornings I think I lifted while I was still sleeping. Even mornings that I felt tired, sore or sick, I still lifted. It always made me feel better about the day and about myself. Like any challenge in life the start is extremely important. Start off small and continue to grow. If making your bed can change the world, think about the effect that all of your other accomplishments can have. It is mind boggling.

Excessive demands on our time have caused an imbalance in our lives because it does not allow us to ever give 100% of our attention and commitment to any given task at a particular time. I explained that life is like the Olympic rings. Each colored ring represents a part of our life. The red circle is your job. The blue circle is your health. The yellow circle is your relationship. The green circle is your financial stability and the black circle is your social life or athletics.

I tell my associates, players and colleges that each circle connects to another circle thereby having a direct effect on the other circles or parts of your life. You have to keep every area of your life going in a positive direction yet focused every day on that activity or activities. I know I have to stay motivated in each area in order to make them all work.

Typically, people are not motivated to change unless given a reason. After all, if it's not broke, why fix it? Well, you might want to fix it if the same old, same old simply isn't working for you any longer, or if you keep trying unsuccessfully to accomplish tasks in the same manner you always have. If you are lacking this motivation externally, create it internally. Incentives work well when we want to accomplish goals. Give yourself rewards for the small achievements to keep yourself motivated to continue on your journey.

For example, most people will motivate themselves to get up every morning and go to work because they know they will be paid and they need the money to pay their bills. The obvious incentive for people to go to school is to get an education, use that education to get a job, and get paid for it. Often I have found that people do not get motivated until the pain of where they are is greater than the pain of where they want to be.

Besides getting a paycheck to pay for the basic necessities of life and fulfil one of our circles in life, many of us want to be a part of something bigger. This in turn keeps yet another of those circles in our lives moving along smoothly. For me, I loved the challenges of work and of coaching. I had to be better than the other sales professionals. I had to win the trip and make the bonus, not because of the money, but because it meant I performed the best.

...en there is the motivation to succeed, to improve and to ... I know I personally am often motivated to do something ...use I enjoy the challenge, or the learning experience. Every ... I take on a new project, I learn more about the subject mat- ...and about myself.

As a coach, it wasn't just about the win. Winning was a ...product of coaching the fundamentals of the game, and the ...ill positions. I also was a fanatic about conditioning. No team ...ould ever be better conditioned than my team both physically and mentally. This was important because it was something that I could control. In life you realize there are so many things you can't control. You quickly learn to control the things you can control because if you don't someone or something else will.

Recognition is something everyone needs and appreciates, but the one thing I always tried to do was be a difference maker to be significant. I was just an ordinary man who tried to accomplish extraordinary things by helping others in their lives and by making a difference in my community. Difference makers, leaders, and role models often share similar qualities: commitment, integrity, courage, determination, and passion. As a difference maker, I was willing to pay the price and positively impact others as I lead by example.

Sometimes having a job to pay the bills is just not enough motivation to remain in a position and do it to the best your ability. Due to many factors, some jobs are no longer fulfilling because you are not making a big enough impact or making a difference.

I had spent 17 years at a major advertising company working my way up the ladder. I had paid more than my price to work my way up the ladder. As I strived to work smarter, I knew I could always work harder than anyone else and I did. Most days I was the first one in and the last one to leave.

Although my former company would never admit it, being a C5/6 quadriplegic confined to a wheelchair negatively impacted my ability to get promoted to higher levels. The perception of someone in a wheelchair getting promoted to the 27th floor of our Michigan Avenue corporate office was not one shared by all the corporate executives. My results had earned me the opportunity, but the interviews always ended with the question of "will he be able to do the job?" One day I was finally given that chance.

At the end of the year I had once again put up top company numbers. I also put up big gains the following year. Despite the recognition, the perks, and six-digit salary the feeling of being fulfilled or making a significant impact were no longer being met by my job. Ultimately, I stepped away from corporate life and started a 501 (C) (3) nonprofit called SOAR. This is what is important to me now.

Always be willing to accept new challenges in life when what you are doing no longer has a significant impact in your life. Change is never easy, but try something new and examine the possibilities. They just might invigorate your mind and spirit with newfound energy and a deeper happiness.

I tell you this with certainty, no matter how much you study, learn and apply your knowledge you cannot create a future worth your time, effort, and energy without faith and a strong relationship with God. Personally, the impact of inspiring and transforming people's lives has been one of the most fulfilling things for me in life.

Self-Reflection

1. Name two (2) accomplishments that you have had in the past year that have your life meaningful.

2. Name three (3) things you do every day or week that helps you move forward.

3. Do you feel content in the current position you hold?

CHAPTER 14

GETTING UP

Getting morale up when times are tough is a skill that is necessary for every team, leader or individual. This ability to pick others up including yourself is a skill necessary for success.

I guarantee that you have been in a situation where either your team, group, peers or yourself have been lacking morale. As you know when you deal with a lack of morale it is an energy drainer. Even if you are full of energy and optimistic, the people who are down or are suffering from bad morale will suck the energy right out of you.

I will tell you the same thing I have instructed others on. When you get in the situation where no one cares, there is no excitement, people feel overwhelmed or not supported and everyone is just doing enough to get by, you will have a choice to make. You can get better or you can get bitter.

Remember if you are in a leadership role, your attitude reflects your leadership and your morale will have a profound effect on the people around you. Everyone must learn how to manage their own morale. If you are a leader, a manager, or an individual who just wants to make a significant impact, you must learn how to get yourself UP!

I have a doctorate degree at getting up and I will share how I keep my morale UP despite spending the past 38 years in a wheelchair as a quadriplegic.

The first thing I do is take several steps to make sure I am in the right mental state to deal with myself or others. I enjoy going on long walks in a park or on a nature path where I try to clear my mind and get away from any stress.

Next, I take some spiritual time to talk to God. Whether from home or in church, I like to thank the good Lord for everything he had blessed me with or ask him to help guide me and give me the strength and wisdom to do what is right.

Another thing I do is to talk to someone I feel can help me keep things in perspective. I have two friends that live out of state that I can call anytime. I know I will laugh and talk smack with and I know when we hang up I will be in a better mind set. They are very honest with me and will tell me when my perspective on things is dead on or give me a different perspective to consider.

Remember you have to keep your morale up in order to help others around you. It is difficult to rise up and be successful when you are being pulled down by bad morale or when you are being drained by those around you. John Maxwell makes a great analogy, "Bad morale is like heavy sandbags on a hot air balloon. You were meant to rise, you were meant to do great things, but it is difficult if not impossible when you are being held down by heavy sandbags."

Bad morale is cancerous and as it spreads can cause a slow death to any business, team or individual. When people feel trapped in a situation and that nothing will ever change because no matter how much they try to change things the environment around them stays the same, people lose hope. Their morale starts to decline and they stop caring. This leads to so many negative behaviors like taking short cuts at work and not giving it your all, to lowering your personal standards like no longer working out or increasing your consumption of alcohol. So how do we ever increase our productivity? Maxwell continues, "As you learn to get rid of these heavy sandbags such as, bad morale, bad attitude, negativity or any other stress factor you will start to rise, and as you rise, you can help others rise too."

There are many other things you can do to lift your morale when suffering from an unpleasant disposition. One of those things is to get moving. You want to get your mind moving and your body moving. When you have activities to occupy your time, your mind has less time to go to a negative place. Create a game plan, write it down, and commit to it.

I tend to push the limits with physical activities when my morale has slipped. I have been known to get into my wheel-chair and go for rides that last for hours. I also go out and hit my punching bag or lift weights while listening to music. When my morale hit a new low after breaking my legs for the second time in four years and having to spend another four months in a hospital bed in my family room, I pushed the physical activi-ties to the limit. Three months after healing I participated in a sprint triathlon. This helped me change my morale. Even though I was nervous about finishing the race, it drove me. I am not recommending it for everyone, but it worked for me. However, if you find it helpful, go for it! I was no longer suffering from low morale.

Some of the other physical things I do you are probably do-ing already, but they really have helped to boost my morale and helped others as well. As I mentioned before, I have a heavy bag hanging in my garage. I also used to have one outside of my of-fice. Yes, it is that simple, I use to beat on the bag until my arms were exhausted. The professionals in my office loved it. And trust me when it got used, production went up.

I have a study in my house that I rarely go use. My wife uses it to do work in and my kids use it to do homework. However, I do go in the study to remind myself of all the difficult times I have dealt with and remind myself of all the successes I have been a part of. There are team awards and recognitions, individual awards, honors, recognitions, trophies and reminders of the extremely difficult times I have conquered. I roll in and just look at the walls and shelves for several minutes and I come out with a renewed spirit and morale.

Knowing what brings your morale up and pulls it down are essential to your life and to the lives of all of the people that you affect every day. It can turn existing into living. Focus on the numerous things that bring you up and avoid the negatives that pull you down. This is a huge weight that we shoulder every day knowing that we are not only responsible for ourselves, but for others. This can become extremely overwhelming and in itself become one of the obstacles that we need to overcome. That is when you have to invest time into yourself! Take time to make it all about you. Do not feel guilty about this. It is a crucial step in the process. It is okay to not look at the big picture for a while, while you are building yourself back up. This will make you a better employee, boss, parent, coach, teammate, leader, or whatever title you hold. This will make you a better you.

Sometimes we all need help. Reach out to get support from those around you to aid in the process of getting UP. People are willing to help, we just have to ask. Talk to family, friends, people from church, or other social groups. There are also many professionals that can guide you through difficult times. Helping others get UP is also a great way to get yourself UP.

I got to this point of my life by absorbing the punches, by developing and embracing traits like commitment, integrity, attitude, self-discipline, GRIT and self-esteem. I believe these are qualities that can be developed. It's not like you get born and die with them. When you want to change, you can, but you must be willing to push yourself mentally, emotionally and spiritually, and then some. I have spent a lifetime developing these traits which, along with the strong influence of my father, empowered me to get through the valleys of depression and defeat.

Part of my mission is to help you turn your obstacles into opportunities. I very often tell people around me to take full responsibility for their lives. The future I am talking about isn't about next year or 20 years down the road. Our time here on earth is so short compared to the eternity we have ahead of us. You have the opportunity to make tomorrow, next week, next year and all of your tomorrows more fulfilling, more rewarding and I implore you to think about what's in your heart.

To foster spiritual growth, it is best to make life simple. To do this, I practice the KIS method, Keep *It Simple*.

> If you're missing someone, call them.
> If you love someone, tell them.
> If you want something, go work for it.
> If you have a question, ask it.
> If you don't like something, try to change it.

This book represents my desire to move forward living a life driven by my higher purpose and my refusal to accept the notion that my disability defines me. The growth in my relationship with God, my faith, and my ability to get UP has been the key.

We are a rugged breed, we quads. If we weren't, we wouldn't be around today. I am a rugged breed in many ways. I have been blessed with a savvy and spirit that isn't given to everyone. Don't underestimate God's power, and His ability to bring healing and restoration in your life. God never promised us a life without pains and struggles, but he did promise to give us strength. Use that strength to get through the difficult times. If you have faith, determination, grit, and the spirit of perseverance, there is no challenge that you can't overcome. You may have to work hard, but the end result will be totally worth it!

Self-Reflection

1. List three things you can do to pick up your morale?

2. Name three things that de-motivate you and what you can do to help remove them?

3. List three things you have done successfully this past year.

NOTES

Louv, Richard. *Last Child in the Woods: Saving Our Children from Nature-Deficit Disorder.* Chapel Hill: Algonquin Press, 2005

Brandt, Paul. *www.thequotablecoach.com* "Don't tell me the sky's the limit when there are footprints on the moon!", 2018

Chapter 1

Covey, Stephen R. *www.famousquotefrom.com* "The price of discipline is always less than the pain of regret." , 2017

Victor, Kiam. *www.brainyquote.com* "Even if you fall on your face, You're still moving forward.", 2018

Coelho, Paulo. *www.quoteambition.com* "What other people think of you is none of your business.", 2018

Edison, Thomas. *www.brainyquote.com* "I have not failed, I've just found 10,000 ways that won't work.", 2018

University of Norte Dame "Play Like a Champion Today."

Chapter 2

Swift, Brian P. *UP Getting Up is the Key to Life.* Mother's House Publishing, 2013

ESPN Saturday College Football Final. Season 2009

Robbins, Tony. *www.brainyquotes.com* "Model someone who is already successful because Success Leaves Clues.", 2018

Emerson, Ralph. *www.goodreads.com* "Once you make a decision, The universe conspires to make it happen.", 2018

Chapter 3

Parker, Sam. 212: *The Extra Degree*. Walk the Talk, 2015

Tzu, Loa. Xplore, *www.brainyquote.com/authors/lao_tzu*, , 2018

Chapter 4

Wilson E.O. Faith Practices; Study Scripture Purposefully World *www.forthillchurch.org*, Oct 1, 2017

Einstein, Albert. *www.quotery.com/quotes/wisdom-is-not-a-product-of-schooling-but-of-the/* "Wisdom is not a product of schooling but of the lifelong attempt to acquire it." , 2018

Knowledge vs. Wisdom *www.dictionary.com* Knowledge is, "acquaintance with facts, truths, or principles, as from study or investigation; general erudition." Wisdom is, "the quality or state of being wise; knowledge of what is true or right coupled with just judgment as to action; sagacity, discernment, or insight." , 2018

Chapter 5

BlueAndGold.com - Lou Holtz At Irish Invasion: Choices Made Dictate Your Path *www.notredame.rivals.com*, 2018

www.newstribune.com/news/news/story/2016/apr/20/lou-holtz...choices/621205/, Apr 20, 2016

Chapter 6

Maxwell, John. *The 15 Invaluable Laws of Growth*, Center Street, 2012

The Empire Strikes Back - Lucas films, 1980

Epictetus: *www.goodreads.com/quotes/738640-we-have-two-ears-and-one-mouth-so-that*, 2018

Chapter 7

Maxwell, John. *The Mentor's Guide to Building a Championship Team, Build a Solid Team, Success vs. Significance,* 2017 audio

ESPN Saturday College Football Final, Season 2008

"Be The Best of Whatever You Are Be Significant!" - Author unknown

Chapter 8

The Creed for the Disabled - Confederate soldier in the Civil War

www.fromthestars.com - Welcome... Beings of Light - Only Two Emotions in the Universe, 2018

Ross, Elisabeth. *www.awakin.org* "There are only two emotions in the universe...love and fear." , 2010

Chapter 10

Ziglar, Zig. *www.brainyquote.com,*"You don't pay the price for success-you pay the price for failure. You enjoy the benefits of success." , 2018

Nike *(slogan)* "Just Do It!"

Maxwell, John - *The Mentor's Guide to Building a Championship Team, Build a Solid Team - Winning as a Team,* 2017 audio

Chapter 11

Tzu, Lau. *www.goodreads.com* "Watch your thoughts; they become words. Watch your words; they become actions. Watch your actions; they become habit. Watch your habits; they become character. Watch your character; it becomes your destiny.", 2018

Ziglar, Zig. *www.brainyquote.com* "You are what you are and where you are because of what has gone into your mind. You can change what you are and where you are by changing what goes into your mind.", 2018

Michael Jordan's Unofficial Guide to Success in the NBA *www.bleacherreport.com*, Feb 14, 2013

Chapter 12

Maxwell, John. *The Mentor's Guide to Building a Championship Team, Build a Solid Team,* 2017 audio.

Chapter 13

Emerson, Ralph Waldo. *www.goodreads.com* "What lies behind us and what lies before us are tiny matters compared to what lies within us.", 2018

www.news.utexas.edu/2014/05/16/mcraven-urges-graduates-to-find-courage-to-change-the-world, 2016

Chapter 14

Maxwell, John. *The Mentor's Guide to Building a Championship Team, Build a Solid Team,* 2017 audio

Maxwell, John. *The 15 Invaluable Laws of Growth,* Center Street, 2012

SUGGESTED ADDITIONAL READING

Godly Men Make Godly Fathers

In the pages of Godly Men Make Godly Fathers, you will meet fathers from diverse upbringings and family structures. You will meet men who have endured significant tests to their faith through tragedy and others who have experienced great triumphs. These fathers will take you on a heartfelt journey. Each chapter tackles a unique viewpoint and is written with unconditional faith and love.

A collection of fathers from across the globe share and implement lessons they learned through their Christian faith to encourage fathers, sons, and families. In this book, these men share their Christian values in hopes of spreading the message of joy, love, and family that transcends race, cultures, and generations.

Up Getting Up is the Key to Life

Up Getting Up is the Key to Life is the creation of the author in which he shares his personal paradigm for mental, emotional, and spiritual recovery while facing the challenges of life as a quadriplegic. It is the author's hope to inspire those with similar injuries and give hope to their medical caregivers, family, and loved ones.

Up Getting Up is the Key to Life is the first book by Brian P. Swift. He writes that recovery consists of healing the mind, not just the body and that recovery is a journey, not a destination. The father of three adopted children and husband of over 28 years, Brian developed his strategy of success, CIA: Commitment, Integrity, and Attitude. With his engaging style and practical wisdom, Brian will leave you invigorated to face your own struggles with hope, faith, and purpose!

The Unofficial Guide to Fatherhood

The Unofficial Guide to Fatherhood: What makes a band of nine fathers want to write a book on fatherhood? They felt a need to share their struggles and successes. In a melody of stories, advice, and experiences, the authors take you on a journey of men who don't hold back their honesty or enthusiasm about being a proud father. You will find moments of joy, sadness, and triumph. Whether you are a father, a mother, son, daughter, or caregiver, there is something in the book for you. It will kindle your excitement to send a message of love.

Go Ask Your Dad

Go Ask Your Dad: A generation of children have heard "Go ask your dad." A culmination of dads from around the country address questions like, How do you raise a daughter? and How do you cope with divorce? to topics like bullying, social-media, forces of terrorism and being a disabled parent. The authors don't claim to be perfect. They do promise, in the book, you will find valuable lessons from their mistakes and successes.

34751106R00080

Made in the USA
Middletown, DE
02 February 2019